CALENDAR COACHING GUIDE

Building A Winning Basketball Team...Month By Month

By Ron Brown

Lessiter Publications, Inc. • Brookfield, WI

Publisher's Cataloging-In-Publication Data

(Prepared by The Donohue Group, Inc.)

Brown, Ron (Ronald George), 1950-
   Calendar coaching guide : building a winning basketball team--
month by month / by Ron Brown.

   p. : ill., charts ; cm.

ISBN: 0-944079-51-2

1. Basketball--Coaching. 2. Basketball--Training. I. Title.

GV885.3 .B76 2006
796.32/3/077

Written by Ron Brown
Edited by Michael Austin
Cover design by Russ Nadasdy
Book design by Geno Coppotelli

International Standard Book Number: 0-944079-51-2

Published by Lessiter Publications, Inc.,
P.O. Box 624, Brookfield, WI 53008-0624.

For additional copies or information on other books or publications
offered by Lessiter Publications, write to the above address.

Telephone: (866) 839-8455 (US Only or Canada) or (262) 432-0388
Fax: (262) 786-5564 • E-Mail: info@lesspub.com
Web site: www.lesspub.com

Manufactured In The United States of America

ACKNOWLEDGEMENTS

First and foremost, I dedicate this book to my father, Douglas H. Brown. Thanks for setting the bar so high, Dad. I love you.

A project of this magnitude only is possible with loving, dedicated and understanding people by your side. First of all, special thanks go out to my lovely wife Shelly, who has proofed, typed and helped with putting together the original manuscript — no small task indeed. Special thanks go out to our young son Nathan, who put up with a working dad during the spring and summer months. I'm sure our oldest boys, Scott and Todd, tired of all the *Calendar Coaching Guide* stories too.

I also would like to thank all the basketball people in my life who saw something in me that warranted their keeping me on their team or helping me with my coaching career. Coach Don Searway guided me in the beginning of church-league ball. Coach Earl Tracy coached my 5th Street Junior High team. Coach Cimbollek, one of Maine's most successful high school basketball coaches always seemed to find the time to sit down with me to offer advice and guidance, especially during my early years.

Special thanks also to Maine's Commissioner of Basketball, Peter Webb, and to John DeRaps, athletic director at Narraguagus High School in Harrington, Maine, for use of specific, school-related material. I'd also like to thank Mike Turner of Turner Sporting Goods in Bangor for his help with specific athletic equipment needs.

I would be remiss if I didn't thank all the doctors and nurses at Eastern Maine Medical Center in Bangor for their kindness and expertise in helping me stay fit and ready for the coaching and writing tasks at hand. I'm indebted to each and every one of them. Special thanks to the staff of the Hemodialysis Center at the hospital — I wouldn't be here without you dear people. And a special thank you to Chaplain Ruth Rooney for her many hours of conversation and inspiration.

I also would like to thank sports editors Joe McLaughlin and Pete Warner from the *Bangor Daily News* for their kindness.

Plus, I must acknowledge all of my former players and assistant coaches who tirelessly listened to the lectures, practice lessons and pep talks through the years. Without them, there would have been no career.

And finally, a word of thanks and appreciation goes out to all the coaches who will take the journey laid out in *Calendar Coaching Guide*. You're in the greatest profession in the world. Never take that task lightly.

INTRODUCTION

Calendar Coaching Guide is a compilation of ideas and concepts, which takes the high school basketball coach on a 13-month journey, outlining month-by-month hints for success in and outside of the gymnasium. There are special sections on teaching offense, defense and special-situation needs. There also are copious forms, diagrams and charts to enhance the teaching and coaching process. Special attention to detail is the overriding point of emphasis.

My goal for the book is to provide coaches a handy, useful tool in the day-to-day operation of their programs. From running a good tryout week to winning the big game, coaches have a month-by-month guide at hand, which helps them prepare for implementing strategies for an entire season and beyond.

I spent a day in 1975 listening to former UCLA mens basketball coach John Wooden speak at a Medalist clinic in Cincinnati, which serves as the inspiration for this book. Since listening to Coach Wooden, I have kept a detailed diary of everything happening in our gym. Now, I can look back a couple of decades and know exactly what we did on a particular day. This proved to be critical when brushing up on my teaching points because as the years go by — one's memory often fades with time.

I also speak to the issue of self-improvement in the *Calendar Coaching Guide*. I was never of the mind at any point in my career that I thought I knew everything. I always entered the off-season attempting to find a clinic, book or magazine article to enhance my program. When I attended a coaching clinic, I thought about wishing to be enlightened by one idea or concept that could make me a better coach and improve my team.

You want to be a better coach and improve your team too. This book can do that. It helps you tie up loose ends while giving a sound base for teaching any area of the game, and perhaps most importantly, re-teaching a specific skill or unit. Success really is in the details and now you have the details at your fingertips. Use these concepts in your practices and you won't be disappointed. In my own coaching career, I always enjoyed practice. Unlike a lot of my colleagues, I never tired of the day-to-day teaching process. This guide provides a nifty way to supplement any teaching style the coach may possess.

Plus, if you're like me, you have compiled an extensive collection of books, videos and other support items to aid yourself and your players. And now, you have a detailed manual that I'm sure is about to become the most important book you have in your coaching library.

FOREWORD

Coaching a winning basketball team doesn't mean picking up a ball in November and turning off the lights in the gymnasium in March. Now, coaches are working 12 months a year and still are trying to find a way to squeeze a 13th month into the calendar (amazingly, this book does just that).

With so much pressure on winning, high school coaches sometimes lose focus of the little things happening throughout the year that make or break a team's success. Conducting a self-evaluation of your coaching skills (May), designing better ways to organize your practices (July) or even taking a vacation to get away from the rigors of the game (August) are small instances where you and your team improve in the off-season.

Coach Ron Brown delves deep into these topics and a host of others in this *Calendar Coaching Guide*. And while the off-season monthly plans are valuable for coaches looking for guidance during the "down" times, Coach Brown details in-season plans as well. Need an offensive philosophy? It's here. Need some time-tested end-of-game plays that are sure to work? It's here too.

I wish there was a book of this depth and substance when I started off my coaching career or during those times when I thought I had the perfect system in place, only to figure out that I wasn't spending my coaching time as wisely as I could have.

Most importantly, Coach Brown speaks from the heart as he has spent 34 years of his life in this noble profession. He's been there on the first day of tryouts. He's been there the night of his players' "biggest game of their lives." And, he's even been there during those long, hot summers when the season seems so far away even though it's sneaking up faster than you can imagine.

The months fly by too quickly these days. The only way to slow them down is through preparation…and the best way to get that preparation is through the *Calendar Coaching Guide*.

—Hubie Brown,
Former NBA Coach,
Current NBA TV Analyst

TABLE OF CONTENTS

TABLE OF CONTENTS

AUTHOR'S PAGE

Calendar Coaching Guide is Ron Brown's sixth basketball-related book. The former CBA coach and NBA talent scout coached junior high, high school, college and professional basketball for 34 years before retiring from teaching and coaching in 2004.

A past president of the Maine Association of Basketball Coaches, Ron was a four-time high school basketball coach of the year in Maine. His teams played for championships 11 times, winning 14 sportsmanship awards in the process. Ron has been inducted into Maine's Sports Legends Hall of Fame (Fall 2006 inductee).

Ron presently is a sports columnist for the *Bangor Daily News* and he's a member of the *Winning Hoops* Advisory Board.

Ron lives in Bangor, Maine, with his wife Shelly and their son Nathan. The couple also has two older sons, Scott and Todd, who now reside out of state. The Brown's three children were named after three former players — all point guards — the coach's favorite position.

Chapter 1

NOVEMBER: THE TEACHING MONTH — ARE YOU READY?

November is the most anticipated month of a high school basketball coach's life. After weeks and weeks of preparation, the tryout week finally is here.

1.1 Pre-Tryout Forms

Open gyms are done; kids are going to sign up to play; and with regular season games approaching, it's time to pick the team and prepare for the hectic, oncoming season. You need to put together the following forms to make the tryout and preseason easier on you and your coaching staff.

FORM 1: Sign-Up Sheet. You'll need basic information from the students planning on trying out for your team (see next page). If you teach in the building, place a couple of sign-up sheets on the wall outside your classroom. If you're not going to be in the building everyday, place these sheets outside the school's main office. If you're in your second year or more at a program, encourage your veteran players to promote not only the location of the sign-up sheets but the tryout itself.

Generally, we like to post our sign-up sheets a couple of weeks before the first night of tryouts. Once you have a good handle on opening-night participants, contact all faculty with a list of those students and inquire about their current academic standing.

FORM 2: Athletic Participant Grade Sheet. Normally, an athletic director or administrator handles contacting the teachers about potential athletes' current academic standing but if that's not the case, try dropping this form (page 11) in each teacher's mailbox.

FORM 3: Emergency Information Sheet. Another important piece of information for the coach and the high school office is the Emergency Information Sheet (page 12). Keep copies in your medicine kits so if you're on the road and a player injury occurs that requires a trip to the hospital, then you have the vital information at hand. Never take anything for granted. Be sure to double- and triple-check with the athletes and their parents or guardians prior to commencing any activity requiring more physical energy than tying sneakers.

After gathering the players' Emergency Information Sheets, take this opportunity to check your medicine-kit supplies. Create a checklist for the following items: instant cold packs, athletic tape, athletic pre-wrap, butterfly bandages, scissors, gauze pads, Band-

Varsity Basketball Sign-up Sheet

Attention all boys (girls) grades 9-12. The first night of tryouts this year will be held Monday night, November 19, from 6:00 - 8:00 p.m. in the high school gymnasium. Please note that all candidates for this year's team will meet briefly at 5:00 p.m. in the cafeteria. Be prompt.

	Name	Grade	Position Played	Address	Telephone Number
1.					
2.					
3.					
4.					
5.					
6.					
7.					
8.					
9.					
10.					
11.					
12.					
13.					
14.					
15.					
16.					
17.					
18.					

1

Aids, Ace bandages, sports injury care handbook, latex gloves, alcohol prep pads, Tuf-Skin, skin lubricant, antiseptic towelettes, tongue depressors, antibiotic creams and finger splints.

1.2 The Tryout

From the vantage point of the head coach, the actual tryout for the team should include skill drills, which can be measured, timed and recorded. Here's a coaching tip — in today's world of accountability, coaches need to have proof of who did what.

Parents usually don't accept the news that their son or daughter isn't good enough to make the squad. If you don't record success or failure in specific areas, then you're likely to hear statements like, "I just spent $160 on new sneakers," or the classic line, "This is the first year my child hasn't made a team." Having back-up material for potential confrontations with those who are cut and their parents always is a good idea.

Athletic Participant Grade Sheet

Name _____

Subject _____

Teacher _____

	Poor	Good	Very Good	Excellent	Comments
Homework					
Quizzes					
Tests					
Other Projects					
Class Participation					
Attitude					
Other Comments					

2

A lot of coaches make the mistake of rolling out the ball, scrimmaging, then picking a team. If your only tool for evaluating talent is scrimmaging, then you are cheating the participants and not giving them a true tryout. Make certain that all participants feel they have a legitimate shot of being on the team. Hurt feelings about being cut during that first week are bad enough. Don't add insult to injury by grouping kids by skill and scrimmaging, then sitting on the sidelines while talking to your staff as the kids scrimmage away all of your tryout time.

Try to time everything in tryouts from speed and success rate of a 3-man weave to wind sprints at the end of each session (Form 4, page 13).

When the scrimmaging portion of the tryout does start, avoid putting too many skilled players together. The cream generally rises to the top in try-out. My old coaching colleague and friend, Carroll Conley, once told me that players usually cut themselves either in tryouts or before the week begins. There's a lot of truth in that axiom, for either in the classroom, or in the gym, non-varsity players often find a way of putting a chance at making the team in jeopardy.

Emergency Information Card

Name _____ Age _____ Date of Birth _____

Address _____

Parent's Name _____ Parent's Phone Number _____

Place of Business _____ Work Phone _____

Cell Phone _____ Other _____

Person to contact in case of emergency _____Phone _____

Illness _____

Special Conditions _____

Other comments _____

_____

Parent or Guardian Signature _____

3

1.3 The Cutting Process

There are a lot of variables that go into selecting a team. During tryouts, coaches should have a good sense of a student's academic standings and each school system varies in its approach to basketball players and grades. In borderline selection situations, the conscientious student has an edge because you don't want to lug less conscientious ones around all year worrying about their grades.

Attitude is a key factor as well. Looking the other way about poor attitude and flattering yourself into thinking you can make this kid change is dangerous. It happens but are you willing to place the welfare of your "project" above the welfare of the entire team? Think about how this situation could play out over the course of the season.

1.4 Final Cut

As a rule of thumb at tryouts, keep all seniors until the final cut. Some of these kids have been with the program four years, so try to give them a close look. It may not be easy but remember, in small schools being cut from the hoop squad can be a traumatic event.

Never keep a freshman or sophomore on your team who will not start or be the first person off the bench. But, look at all kids on the first night (grades 9-12). Then, keep underclassmen who can help you. Kids mature more quickly than they used to and some 9th and 10th graders are ready earlier for the high school team than they might have been 20 years ago. The proliferation of strength exercises and the training that goes with it, AAU and YBOA club teams, and, of course,

Timed Drills/Results

Name	3-Man Weave	Chair Dribble	Full-court Dribble & Return	Zig-Zag	Mikan Drill	Free Throws	Suicides
Smith, John							
Jones, Walton							
White, Bill							
Wilkes, Stan							
Brown, Nate							
Strout, Jaxon							
Worcester, Cory							
Cyr, Nate							

4

advanced training kids receive in summer camps all factor into that decision.

1.5 How To Deliver The News

There's no correct or incorrect way to deliver the news of who did and didn't make the team. You can post final rosters, call kids who made the cut or bring each player into your office to tell them individually if they made the squad or not. My preference is informing all kids face-to-face but it can be time-consuming. Never underestimate the impact your final decision has on a young life. Never.

After informing the players, it's time to inform the faculty (Form 5, next page). Teachers appreciate knowing athletic rosters and that you are interested in keeping abreast of grades, classroom behavior and attitude. Communicating with faculty is easier if you are a teaching member of the school but if you are not, be sure to take the time to let school staff know who is on the team. It doesn't have to be an in-depth form of communication, just follow the sample letter.

The teaching staff at the high school is vital to any success you and your team may have. The young boys or girls who make up the varsity basketball team should be told that it is a privilege to be on that squad. Teach them that they are now under the spotlight of public recognition.

1.6 Starting The Process

Once the teams are picked and once the rosters have been distributed, it's

November 23, 2004

Dear Faculty,

I am happy to introduce to you this year's boys varsity basketball team.

Please know that these young gentlemen (ladies) are expected to exhibit exemplary behavior on and off the basketball floor for the entire period that they represent our school as athletes.

Sincerely,

Ron Brown
Head Coach

12	11	10	9
Jones, Walton	Smith, John	Brown, Nate	Cyr, Nate
Strout, Jason	White, Bill	Worcester, Cory	Barnes, Steve
Flagg, Jack	Wilkes, Stan		
Sills, Peter	Cote, Ned		
	Jordan Franks		

5

time to take the kids to "class" and begin the arduous process of putting the team together. Begin each year by giving each player a simple playbook. While simple spiral notebooks are fine, I've found the more elaborate loose-leaf notebooks work better. Doll them up with a school sticker on the cover, which prominently displays your team's mascot or logo. This playbook is critical, especially in the preseason when it's a good idea to spend two or three 1-hour sessions with your players going over everything from half-court offensive sets to full-court presses.

Other forms to include are the season schedule (times and locations), a calendar featuring what happens on each day of the week and at what time (i.e. boys' practice from 2:30-5, girls' practice from 5-7), equipment issue form (so you know what kind of gear was issued to each player and when it was issued), a basketball contract and goal cards. Kids are proud to have a playbook under their arms when they walk into

class. Always preach to them how fortunate they are to be part of such a team as the varsity basketball team.

1.7 The Contract

The contract is a key instrument in establishing trust between the player and the coach. Ask each parent to read and sign the document before the player returns it. Here's how our contract reads:

GENERAL OBJECTIVES

This contract is made between coach and player to help make the player aware that the basketball season revolves around the philosophy of unity and responsibility to the group and that the system must be set up to make the player understand the need for structure and that violations of policies will result in his removal from the squad. The season becomes a continuous tryout where the emphasis on cohesion to a unit is stressed to the athlete.

This contract is further established

14

in order to inculcate good sportsmanship, respect for rules and authority, to attain and maintain physical and mental fitness, to establish leadership, to establish team pride, to establish teamwork, to establish team discipline, and to discourage disruptive influences in the locker room, on the court, off the court and on school-related trips.

SPECIFIC OBJECTIVES

1. To help the athlete become responsible to his or her teammates.

2. To help the athlete become aware of the need for following the training policies of the coach.

3. To help the athlete become aware of the need for following team policies.

4. To help the athlete set goals and attain them through following these policies.

5. To help the athlete become accountable to himself in the attainment of his or her goals.

THE TRAINING RULES

1. No use of alcoholic beverages in any form. Violation of this training policy will result in immediate removal from the squad.

2. No use of tobacco. Same regulations apply.

3. No use of drugs in any form, other than given by a doctor's approval. The above regulations apply.

4. Curfews will be set up throughout the course of the season. If the player violates curfew at any time, he destroys the trust that has been given to him. He must realize the importance of good health as a necessary factor in his success. The WEEK NIGHT curfew of 11 p.m. will simply mean the athlete will be in his place of residence at that hour. This curfew will apply to any week night and any night prior to a contest,

example: a Saturday tournament game. Also, a WEEKEND curfew of midnight is in place. If curfew is violated: a) first offense: 1-game suspension; b) second offense: 2-game suspension; and c) third offense: dismissal.

TEAM POLICIES

1. The athlete WILL NOT play basketball during the course of the season unless he is under the supervision of the coach. Penalty: 1-game suspension.

2. Unexcused absences from practices or games: If for medical and family reasons the athlete will miss practice or games, he must contact the coach, preferably through his parent. If practice is missed, or a game is missed, without prior approval or the coach's knowledge: a) first violation: 3 days suspension; b) second violation: 1 week suspension; and c) third violation: dismissal.

3. Tardiness for practice: In order for the athlete to gain full benefits from the program, he must be prompt to team meetings and practices: a) first violation: 1 lap per minute late; b) second violation: 2 laps per minute late; c) third violation: 3 laps per minute late; d) fourth violation: 4 laps per minute late; e) fifth violation: 5 laps per minute late; f) sixth violation: 1 game suspension; and g) seventh violation: dismissal.

DATE_____

I, _____, agree to abide by the rules as stated. I realize violations of these policies hurt the team and the program.

Coach's signature:_____

Parent's signature:_____

1.8 Goal Cards

Two sets of goal cards should be made: individual goals and team goals. For the individual goal cards, the player's name, year in school and position is listed. On the back are the player's goals for the season, for example: "I would like to improve my dribble with my opposite hand. I need to work on my defense and speed. In doing so, I hope to become a starter and contribute more to the team."

The team goal card carries the same information on the front of the card, then lists the player's team goals for the season on the back, for example: "I would like to see us win at least 13 games this year and be in the top 4 in our division. I think we have what it takes to go all the way. We need to play our game and be patient. The states would be the ultimate goal!"

Season Goals

1. Win all sportsmanship awards offered by the referees, our conference, and state principals' association in the postseason.
2. Hold our opponents to less than 50 points per game every night.
3. Average 65 points or more every game.
4. Shoot at least 50% from the floor every night.
5. Shoot 70% or better from the foul line every night.
6. Win our conference title.
7. Qualify for the postseason.
8. Avoid a playoff game by finishing in the top five in our division.
9. Be regarded by every opponent we play as the toughest team they face.
10. Enjoy each other's company and have fun.

6

Team Goals

OFFENSE GOALS
1. Average 65 points or better.
2. Shoot 50% from the floor.
3. Shoot 70% from the line.
4. Concentrate on good shots.
5. Make 75% of shots in the paint.
6. Shoot 33% from 3-point range.

DEFENSE GOALS
1. Hold the opponent under 50 points each night.
2. No "star" gets more than 15 points per game.
3. No big first period, score-wise.
4. Clamp down after halftime.
5. Keep opponent's shooting percentage under 40%.
6. Talk as a unit, regardless of our defense: half-, 3/4- or full-court.

7

1.9 Specific Goals

Specific goals such as goals for the head coach, team goals by game and offensive and defensive goals are important to note as well.

This stuff can be a headache but the key here is to perform these mundane, preseason tasks in a sit-down session or two, away from the gym. Don't cut practice time with this stuff. Prudent coaches take their teams to a classroom to save valuable practice time for teaching and preparing for the season.

1.10 Make Your Half-Court Offense Work

Regardless of what you wish to do to get your players in shape for what lies ahead, begin teaching from Day 1. Sometimes, depending on the situation, you may find yourself teaching during tryouts.

Some coaches fashion themselves as

defensive gurus and teach nothing but defense the first week or two. They have the mindset of, "We never touch a ball the first two weeks." I like playing those people early. We prefer that our first teaching unit is our half-court, man-to-man offense.

Knowing the following strict details and paying strict attention to them keep most offenses running smoothly and provide teams with a more effective system, which leads, ultimately, to the goal of winning.

Detail No. 1 — Know the offense inside and out before teaching it. As simple as it sounds, a lot of problems evolve in half-court sets primarily because the instructor (you) isn't familiar with the many nuances of the offense. Don't get tricked into thinking you can employ something you've seen on television or while you were out scouting. A good place to begin your lesson in offense is to read. That means going to online coaching services, subscribing to coaching publications and reading books on the fundamentals of half-court sets all the way to special situational work.

Detail No. 2 — Do you have the correct personnel to run the set? Far too many coaches try to get kids to do something they are incapable of doing. Coaches need to be honest with their teams and themselves. Running a perimeter-orientated offense with a club clearly needing to be an inside-orientated team causes problems for the coach and the players.

Detail No. 3 — Teach your offense through drills. A lot of coaches make the mistake of walking their players through an offense, then expecting them to perform it. Key areas such as spacing go by the boards, players get

confused and the whole system breaks down. Each key area of the set needs to be broken down into drill form. Things progress more smoothly with this method.

Detail No. 4 — Dummy your set(s) every night. An underrated coaching tool is dummying. Dummying is running through your offense without defense and without scoring. Players need to get all of this into their subconscious to be effective on the floor. Players come back who played for us years ago still can run our stuff because of this tool. Realistically, we spend 10-15 minutes a day dummying our sets. A helpful hint: substitute your normal pattern of player entry in this drill too. And, penalize kids who get confused by having them run a lap or two for a miscue. That minor penalty enhances concentration.

Detail No. 5 — Spend more time in the half-court than the full. Scrimmage less and work your offenses and defenses in the half-court. Your team becomes a better man-to-man team if you spend more time in the half-court. There are plenty of uses for full-court work, including getting and keeping your team in shape, which is a must early in the season. But, let's face it, big games are won by teams that are efficient with their half-court offenses.

Detail No. 6 — Offenses vs. man-to-man defense. My teams enjoyed their best seasons by combining a motion offense with rules, a number of set plays and a continuity pattern, which ultimately keeps any defense honest. Single-coverage defense should pose no psychological or physical problem for a team's thinking offensively.

Detail No. 7 — Teaching motion offense. Texas Tech's Bob Knight deserves the credit for getting a coaching community fired up about motion offense during his early days of coaching at Indiana University. Since then, a number of variations on this offense have been born. Today, it's tough to walk into any gym and not see some form of motion offense being run. Our team prefers a 3-2 set, which is outlined in Diagram 1.

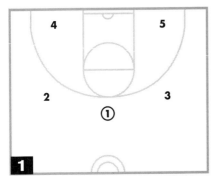

DIAGRAM 1: 3-2 Set. 1, the point guard, is the team's best ball handler and floor leader. 2 is a decent shooting off-guard. 3 is the same as 2 but also may serve as a small forward. 4, ideally, is a big forward. 5 is the team's center or post player. The rules for this set are simple. 1 signals for motion offense (a hand signal from the bench easily can be relayed to 1). Once players hustle into position, 2 makes a V-cut to get free for a pass from 1.

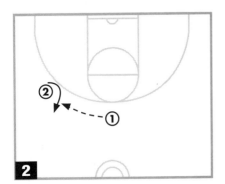

DIAGRAM 2: V-Cut. 2 makes a V-cut and receives the pass from 1.

DIAGRAM 3: Initiate Motion. After releasing the ball, 1 sets a cross-screen for 3 to initiate the motion principles of the offensive set. 3 uses the screen to take the position of 1.

DIAGRAM 4: In Motion. 3 receives a pass from 2. 3 takes a shot or makes a move to the basket.

DIAGRAM 5: Front-Court

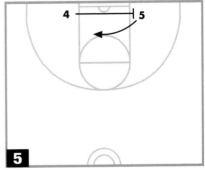

Motion. Recipients of the initial pass in the 3-2 set are instructed to look at 4 and 5 to see how they are being played by their defenders. 4 or 5 should not remain stationary for more than three passes on the perimeter, otherwise their only function becomes one of rebounding. Get the big players moving immediately. In the diagram, 4 screens for 5. When screening, 4 runs at the defender and stops. 4's hands should be at his crotch so he doesn't push the defender. 4 must remain stationary when making the screen. 5's objective is to cut then stop three-quarters of the way across the lane. No rule of this offense is more important than that. Cutting across the entire lane causes 5 to be in a position too far from the basket. When cutting, 5 holds his inside hand high to provide a good target for a pass.

DIAGRAM 6: Entry Pass. 2 passes to 5. Remember your team's strengths when running the motion offense. If you have strong post players, this pass works perfectly. However, if your team's strength is perimeter shooting, use the post players to employ back picks to free shooters.

DIAGRAM 7: Back Pick. 4 screens for 2, which opens up space for a move to the basket or a shot.

Keep in mind flexibility when teach-

ing the motion offense. Players who end up at the point or wing in the set (this includes post players as well), must be on the lookout for isolated teammates on the low block.

Instruct players at all times to maintain floor balance in the offense. Another significant point is the spacing of players. Motion offenses, like any others, get bogged down if players are aligned too closely together. A good rule of thumb is to instruct players always to be 15-18 feet apart from each other. If not, then the defense has the advantage.

DIAGRAM 8: Pass Into Block. If post players are good at getting position, send an immediate pass into the block. For example, 2 passes to 4. For the sake of argument, say 4 has a nice baby hook shot. If the players and coach know this and the 3-2 is taught properly, smart

players within the set should look to utilize each other's strengths.

Detail No. 8 — Set plays to enhance the offense. Once coaches are comfortable with their players in the 3-2 motion offense, the next step is to add set plays against man-to-man defense to enhance or elaborate what the motion offense gives their team. The key to offensive success in the half-court is to lull the defense into a false sense of security. Have a lot of what you run in the half-court start out and look the same, then move to a different direction to something else, and hopefully, a quick basket.

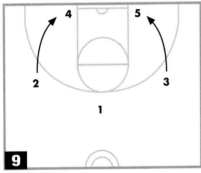

DIAGRAM 9: Stack Set. To change things in your motion offense, go to a stack by having 2 and 3 move behind 4 and 5.

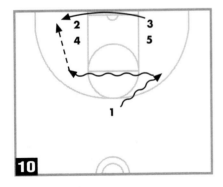

DIAGRAM 10: Motion In Stack.

1 establishes the side of the floor with a dribble and by doing so keys the initial move of the offense. 3 flashes the baseline behind the automatic double-screen formed by the union of 2 and 4. Often times, 3 is open for the shot.

DIAGRAM 11: Foul-Line Flash. A shot for 3 isn't the only look as 2 comes to the foul line. 2 gets a lot of open shots from this motion because of the confusion created. 3 also can look into the post for 4 on the block.

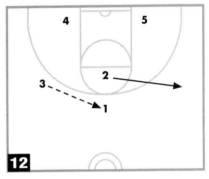

DIAGRAM 12: Back To Motion. If there is a breakdown in a set play, the players return to the motion set. 3 passes back to 1 at the point and 2 moves from the foul line to the other wing. Teams need to practice the stack regularly because of the many nuances it opens up other than the initial-series looks outlined here. Point guard clear-

outs are a significant option off the stack alignment. Also be aware of the significance of a two-man game resulting in a stack set.

Keep in mind the importance of understanding one's personnel and their subsequent abilities prior to entering into any teaching relationship with any offensive alignment. We use forms to rate our guards, forwards and centers based on 10 skills for each. We rate them on a scale of 1-10 (1=poor, 10=best) for each skills. For example, for guards, rate dribbling, passing, seeing the floor, pass off the dribble, shoot off the dribble, leadership qualities, shooting ability, courage under fire, eye contact and strength of off-hand. For forwards, rate triple threat, passing, dribbling, shooting, attitude, desire, can play other positions, seeing the floor, rebounding and strength of off-hand. Rate centers on playing with back to the basket, passing, rebounding, seeing the floor, blocks out well, type of teammate, shot blocker, off-hand skills, variety of shots and toughness in traffic.

Detail No. 9 — A Continuity Offense. The continuity offense plays into the same philosophy of running a different offense out of our initial motion set to lull the defense into a false sense of confidence.

DIAGRAM 13: Boomerang Effect. 1 passes to 3 (this can run to the opposite side as well, just move the entire motion to the opposite side). 1 cuts to 3's side. 3 dribbles the ball to the middle and 5 moves up to replace 3. As this happens, 1 cuts to the middle. 2 and 4 exchange positions. The continuity of the set is simple. Once run through one time, the offense returns to its initial look with players in different spots.

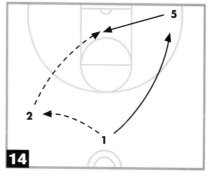

DIAGRAM 14: End-Game Offense. To utilize the 3-2 continuity as an end-of-game offense, move all players out 10 feet from their original position. If protecting a lead, get your better ball handlers into the game at this time. In a stalling mode, teach your players to continue the normal rudiments of the offense but always look for the easy basket. 1 looks for inside opportunities for himself as a cutter or for a pass to 2, who can hit 5 on a quick cut to the basket.

When teaching your players the 3-2 motion-in-motion continuity pattern, go with a simple mantra and yell it during the initial instruction of the series: "Pass to the side. Cut to that side. Opposite players exchange positions." Enhance that verbal instruction by getting players to concentrate on keeping

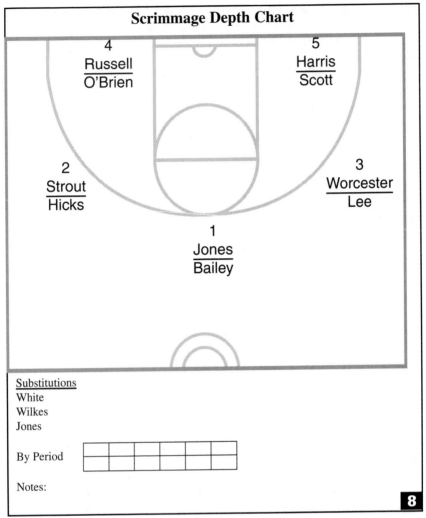

Scrimmage Depth Chart

4
Russell
O'Brien

5
Harris
Scott

2
Strout
Hicks

3
Worcester
Lee

1
Jones
Bailey

Substitutions
White
Wilkes
Jones

By Period

Notes:

8

the ball in the middle of the floor, especially when the 3-2 is used as an end-game mechanism.

1.11 Make Your Preseason And Exhibition Games Productive

An important element of preseason work is scrimmaging and playing exhibition games. A scrimmage occurs when two different teams play in the preseason with little regard for time or score. After we've picked our team, we practice for a week or so, then scrim-

mage an opponent (either home or away). Both coaches agree on the setup but try to play at least six 8-minute periods, erasing the score after each 16-minute session.

Exhibition games are a horse of a different color. Try to play at least one or two 32-minute "games" before opening the season. Exhibitions attempt to simulate real-game conditions.

Whether it's a scrimmage or exhibition game, every squad member should see some playing time. Not every player is going to see a lot of time in every regular season game although try to reward all squad members for their hard work. But, in a preseason game, squad unity is hurt when the coach limits who plays to just a select few. Be sure each player gets some quality time and not just a 45-second appearance at the end of a half.

These scrimmages and exhibitions allow you to work with different player combinations as well. Some players are more willing to give themselves up than others are. Get one of your assistants or managers to write down all your experimental combinations.

Create a depth chart for a scrimmage or exhibition game (Form 8, previous page). Knowing who played when you excelled on offense or defense is a key in determining who are your starters and bench players heading into the season. This also allows you to keep groups of five together instead of playing just seven or eight players for most of the scrimmage, then emptying your bench. Try to play a true back-up second string that matches up position by position.

Other ways to better utilize preseason games is to rotate reserves by position. Create game conditions in your team's mind so they adjust to them at this point in the season to be ready for regular-season games. For example, pull your starting center early and replace him with the back-up center to simulate foul trouble for your starting post player.

Another philosophy to incorporate into your scrimmages is to shoot all fouls. If you're in an opponent's gym and you're not shooting all fouls (shooting fouls or not), that affair is going to be rough. That allows your opponent to hack your players without penalty and it teaches your team bad defensive habits as there is no consequence for fouls.

Work on special situations against an opponent as well in preseason games. Don't worry so much about score and concentrate on taking advantage of working on time situations such as end-game scenarios with a clock running, officials officiating and people in the stands.

1.12 Understanding Defense

Any discussion of defense at the high-school level must begin with the teaching of man-to-man defense. It is important from the outset of teaching for the coach fully to understand what his or her team is capable of doing at the defensive end of the floor.

There are several philosophies on defense. Some coaches really set no parameters of success for their teams other than scoring one more point than the opposition. You may not be as liberal in your defensive thinking (I'm not), so it's important to set limits and preach these goals to your players. Nothing motivates a team more at the defensive end of the floor than to strive for a goal – translated into a number of points – then reach it by the end of the game.

In my high-school program we liked to keep the opposition at 49 points or less for a 32-minute contest. Sound ridiculous? It's not, really. One year we held the opposition to less than 40 points per game. Like anything else you teach and preach in the gym, playing good defense becomes a mindset. As a coach, I never was convinced that there was a single player on any team I had who could not play man-to-man defense. Granted, there were match-up problems from time to time with certain players versus other but coaching adjustments are part of the game.

You need to enter the teaching process of any defensive unit by stressing to those players the significance of a particular defense to the program's chance for success. Begin by emphasizing the importance of playing man-to-man defense. No zone defense, of any variety, is taught successfully and administered unless the players are blessed with the knowledge of single-coverage, man-to-man defense.

Lately, it seems that match-up zones have become all the rage in coaching. I had the good fortune a number of years ago to spend some time with the match-up zone guru Bill Green. We brought Coach Green to Maine to speak at a coaches' clinic and a short time later the celebrated Marion High School hoop coach from Indiana and I were on the same clinic staff in Minnesota. Coach Green's philosophy of the match-up defense centers around solid man-to-man defensive principles. Match-ups are much more effective than regular zone defenses, especially if players are well-schooled in man-to-man principles.

Under the blanket heading "defense," there are several teaching areas to consider. Refer to Forms 9-16 for quick references in regard to a variety of basic defensive situations.

Teaching Area No. 1 — Single-Coverage Defense. The best place to begin is instructing players how to guard the man with the ball (Form 9). Proper stance and positioning are vital roles for players if they're going to be successful playing this type of defense.

The most important thing for players to understand is the role balance plays

Guarding The Player With The Ball

Note these seven areas when instructing a defender on guarding the player with the ball.

1. Proper stance.
2. Balance.
3. Comfort.
4. Lead with either foot forward.
5. Body weight on front foot.
6. Left hand up for right-hand dribbler/shooter.
7. Right hand up for left-hand dribbler/shooter.

Notes:

9

in defense. One of my pet peeves about defensive instruction centers around players who are taught to be too low to the ground while addressing their opponent. Strive to teach balance and comfort within the so-called stance to your players.

It also is vital to teach different situations to players. There's a world of difference between guarding the shooter in the 3-point area and defending the post player.

Instruct players to move forward out of the aforementioned position once the dribbler begins his move. Keep defenders in the defensive position three feet away from the ball-handler. On the perimeter, have your players sag slightly, not yet completely on top of the opponent. Instruct your players to move forward out of the aforementioned position once the dribbler begins his move.

The defender moves closer to the player dribbling the ball but still is not completely on his man (Form 10, next page). He remains about an arm's length away. It is vital that players are taught not to play their opponents too

Guarding The Player Dribbling The Ball

Note these four areas when instructing a defender guarding the player who is dribbling the ball.

1. Defender moves closer
2. Not completely up on the dribbler – arm's length away
3. Don't play too tightly – especially on the perimeter
4. Know the opponent's perimeter shooting ability – adjust accordingly

Notes:

10

Guarding The Man Who Has Pulled Up His Dribble

Note these five areas when instructing a player guarding the man who has pulled up his dribble.

1. Bury the dribbler
2. Hands straight up in the air
3. Not reaching or hacking
4. If ball is loose, go for it
5. Otherwise, hands stay home

Notes:

11

Guarding The Opponent One Pass Away

Note these five areas when instructing a player guarding the player one pass away from the ball.

1. Place yourself between opponent and ball
2. Keep the defensive triangle, ball-you-opponent
3. Never take eyes off the ball
4. Overplay without side hand up
5. Don't hold opponent or impede progress with other hand

Notes:

12

Guarding The Opponent Two Passes Away

Note these five areas when instructing a player guarding the player two passes away from the ball.

1. Keep the defensive triangle
2. Step in to the lane area
3. Both hands extended as wide as possible
4. Feet are balanced and even
5. Weight is evenly distributed
6. Talk to defenders out front

Notes:

13

tightly, especially on the perimeter. Players also must be instructed not to sag too much on the perimeter. Once the offensive player begins the dribble move, sagging too much leads to a quick score.

When the dribbler ceases to dribble, teach your players to "bury" the opponent (Form 11). The defender is aggressive but not committing a violation.

To defend the player who is one pass away (Form 12), teach your unit that any player who is capable of receiving a pass or becoming part of the offense with the next pass necessitates defense, which is essentially denial defense. The defender is to place himself between his man and the ball and never take his eyes off the ball. In this instance, overplay the point man.

Offensive players who cannot receive the ball from teammates with less than two passes generally are guarded in the lane (Form 13). Here, call on the defensive triangle so defenders off the ball are in ideal positions to aid their teammates.

A wrinkle to this overall defensive philosophy is that it is more geared at on-the-ball coverage at all positions. Although there are some situations requiring denying the ball, this defense stresses more of a sagging man coverage with a special emphasis on popping out on the opponent once he receives the ball. We've found when playing teams that deny every pass on every possible possession, it's easy to back-door them to death. Set plays like the stack series especially are effective against denial defense. Driving those defenders lower than they'd like to be puts the pressure on the other defenders on the floor. Denial-type coaches like to push the ball to the sidelines. Our

---

Guarding The Post

Note these five areas when instructing a player guarding a player on the block.
1. Squared stance or "wrestler's" stance
2. Man-to-man rules apply for opponent with basketball
3. Stay behind the opponent
4. Don't reach, hack or slap
5. Don't lean on the opponent to gain an advantage

Notes:

14

---

defense stresses clogging the middle.

A vital part of man-to-man defensive instruction is teaching players how to defend the low-post player and the low-post area (Form 14). Spend a lot of practice time breaking down defensive assignments into one-on-one play, two-on-two play and three-on-three play.

For post coverage, teach your defenders (anyone can end up covering a player in the post) never to attempt a shot block until the offensive player has released the basketball (Form 15). An age-old axiom with referees and shot blockers centers around officials'

Shot Blocking

Note these six areas when instructing your players on the proper way to block a shot.
1. Don't reach
2. Don't anticipate
3. Don't attempt a block until the basketball is out of the opponent's hands
4. Attempt to block the ball and keep it inbounds
5. Block the ball to a teammate, if possible
6. Block the ball to yourself, if possible

15

---

anticipation of fouls on shot-block attempts. If the defender waits until the ball is out of the shooter's hands, very few, if any, fouls are called.

Rushing the point guard to attempt a steal on a return pass from the wing to

---

Defensive No-No's

Note these five defensive no-no's when working on defensive drills in practice, so these rules are followed when it comes to playing games.
1. Avoid rush steals from the point on passes from the wing.
2. Respect the point guard's shooting ability — always
3. Avoid wildly overplaying passes to the wing
4. Never turn your back on the ball
5. Don't front the post unless the passer's dribble has been buried

Notes:

16

---

the point usually results in a wide-open look for the player whose defender has just rushed by. Overplaying passes to the wing usually results in back-door lay-ups, especially if the defender doesn't keep the defensive triangle previously discussed.

If you want your low-post players to front their men, then the point and wing defenders must bury the dribblers, otherwise it's an easy maneuver for the ball-handler to lob a pass into the post (Form 16, previous page).

As this chapter concludes, here are a few more ideas on some forms to create for this time of year. First, chart your players' free-throw shooting in practice. Keep track of attempts and makes. Also, have a form where you type out what your practice plans are for that day of the week. Jot everything down and even drop in some ideas on future plans. For example, figuring out who is your best point guard, who needs more defensive work or developing role players to come off your bench.

This chapter ends with a sample practice plan (Form 17). Keep everything on a schedule as normally you have about two hours to accomplish your day's work.

Sample November Practice Plan

Varsity Boys Basketball Practice Plan (2 hours)

2:30-2:37	Stretch
2:37-2:45	Free shoot
2:45-2:55	Pre-game (normal warm-ups)
2:55-3:05	3-man weave
3:05-3:15	Five laps — water break
3:15-3:25	25 free throws
3:25-3:30	Brief discussion with team
3:30-3:45	Teach the offense
3:45-4:00	Teach the defense
4:00-4:15	Half-court scrimmage
4:15-4:25	Special situations
4:25-4:30	Sprints
End of practice	

Notes:

17

COURT TERMINOLOGY & POSITIONS

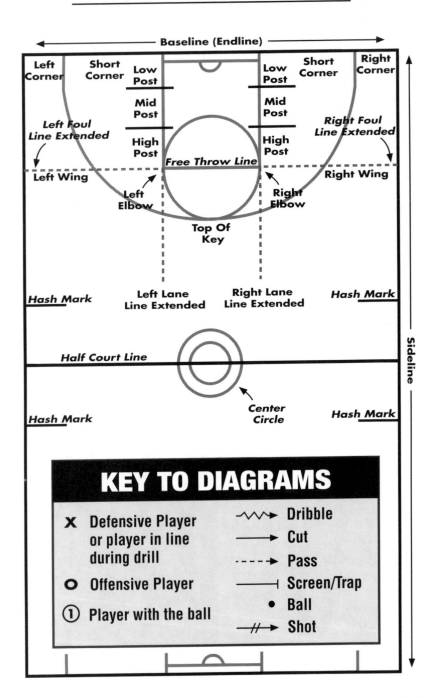

◄────────── **Baseline (Endline)** ──────────►

Left Corner Short Corner Low Post Low Post Short Corner Right Corner

Mid Post Mid Post

Left Foul Line Extended *Right Foul Line Extended*

High Post **Free Throw Line** High Post

Left Wing Right Wing

Left Elbow Right Elbow

Top Of Key

Left Lane Line Extended **Right Lane Line Extended**

Hash Mark *Hash Mark*

Half Court Line

Sideline

Hash Mark **Center Circle** *Hash Mark*

KEY TO DIAGRAMS

X Defensive Player or player in line during drill	⌇⌇⌇►	**Dribble**
	───►	**Cut**
	----►	**Pass**
O Offensive Player	───┤	**Screen/Trap**
① Player with the ball	•	**Ball**
	─//►	**Shot**

CALENDAR COACHING GUIDE

Chapter 2

DECEMBER: LET THE GAMES BEGIN

Most teams have a week or so in December to continue the teaching process. By that point, you have given your team a sound base to open the season. Prior to beginning more teaching this month, ask your coaches to set goals for the season, individual games, offense and defense. Get these goals down in writing from your assistants, junior varsity coach and ninth-grade coach.

2.1 Extending The Defense

To better explain each of the defensive calls in this section, I'll use the calls and names we used in our program on the defensive side. When in a half-court, man-to-man defense, this is a 5 defense, signaled by the coach holding up his hand, palm facing out indicating that five players are guarding five players. When deciding to pick up the guards at the 10-second line, this is the 52 defense.

DIAGRAM 1: 52 Defense. The 52 defense is a bother defense. Move to this coverage early in the game to see what the opposition does versus extended pressure. A lot of time, the opposition gets the ball in the wrong hands, so to speak, and a turnover is forced. High school coaches, especially new coaches, are surprised by how quickly a turnover results from such a simple move.

DIAGRAM 2: 53 Defense. The 53 defense is a 3/4-court extended man-to-man defense. This diagram show a two-man trap out of the 53 when 1 passes to 2, X2 stays on 2 and X1 hustles to trap. The 53 defense requires denial by the other defenders on the court while there is no denial in the 52 defense.

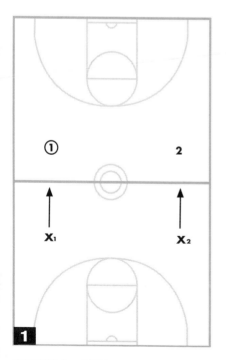

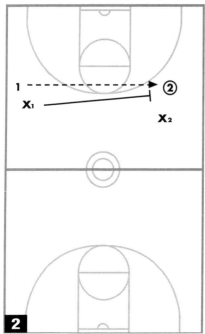

2

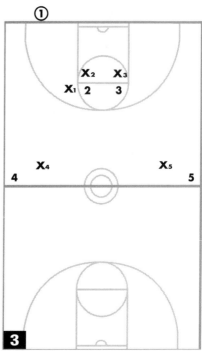

3

This is where scouting the opponent comes into play. If you're about to play an opponent who possesses, at best, a fair point guard, then you know that by getting the ball in other people's hands, you create trouble for the other team. The 53 defense capitalizes on your opponent's offensive dilemma immediately. Or, now you can move to the 54 defense (run-and-jump), which is a full-court, man-to-man defense.

2.2 Teaching The Run-And-Jump

DIAGRAM 3: 54 Defense. Leave the inbound passer alone in the 54 defense. In most cases in man-to-man press offenses the opponent's best ball-handler usually is the inbound passer. In the 54, double-team the next best ball-handler (2), which in theory gets the basketball to the opponent's third best ball-handler.

From a strict percentage standpoint, this defensive move increases your success in the 54 defense. The third-best ball-handler often lobs the ball into trouble simply to avoid a violation, after all, these high school players are only human and being embarrassed is never something they strive to do. Also, teach your players that the 54 press is often most effective when you don't get a turnover at all. A lot of times, you get just what you want from the press by forcing the opponent to take a poor shot versus this defense.

DIAGRAM 4: Running & Jumping. Say the inbound pass gets to the third-best ball-handler (3), statistics show that if the inbound passer is right-handed, the initial inbound pass goes to his right (next page). This is when your defense makes its move and begins the running and jumping part of the philosophy. When 3 catches the ball, X2 runs to recover and guard him. X4 leaves

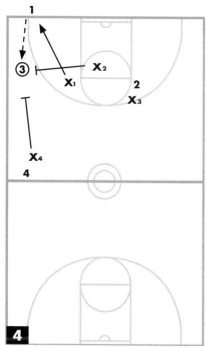

4

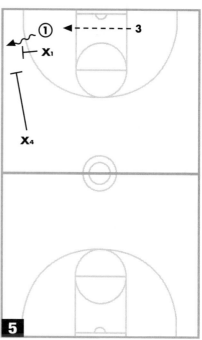

5

his player to jump the ball-handler. 3 wants to get the ball back 1 but by this point the inbounder should be covered by X1 and denied the opportunity to receive the pass.

DIAGRAM 5: Forcing Sideline. If 3 gets the pass to 1's left, most likely he wants to get it immediately back to 1. After 1 receives the pass back from 3, X1 forces him toward the sideline and X4 comes further into the backcourt to create a double-team. In the run-and-jump, alter your defensive philosophy somewhat from what was taught in the 5 defense. In the 5, look to push the action toward the middle but in the run-and-jump, force the players to the sidelines. The one critical thing to teach your defenders is that when trapping, someone obviously is left alone.

There are some keys to remember when playing the running-and-jumping style in the 54. First, when trap-

ping, someone always is open. Your team must be quick, react well and hustle at all times. Plus, basket coverage always is critical. You'd rather have a failed jump maneuver than leaving the basket unguarded. If your center has a choice between trapping and being the last man back to cover the hoop, he must retreat.

Another coaching tip is that the 10-second line is your line of retreat in all full-court presses. If the defense allows the ball to get to the 10-second line, then it's time to retreat and play half-court defense. Finally, when coaching the 54 defense in practice, use six or seven offensive players to attack the press to teach defenders to hustle, move and anticipate passes.

2.3 Teaching Zones

The decision to play zone defense involves several factors, most importantly, knowing what players are capable of performing is of the utmost relevance. Big, sluggish teams or when you have to play a larger squad are both times when zone can be effective.

Coaches choose many different points in a game to use a zone, like after a missed shot, when leading the game (especially after a good stretch of man defense) or just to mix it up.

We stick with two or three zone looks and always play an even-front zone when the opponent is inbounding the ball underneath his basket.

2.4 The 2-1-2 Defense

The 2-1-2 (we called it 21) is an ideal defense to hide players who are in foul trouble, especially big players you need in the game. Also, if the opponent is a little quicker than your team but not a great shooting squad, a 2-1-2 is a good choice.

DIAGRAM 6: 2-1-2 Defense. X1 and X2 are guards while X3, X4 and X5 are the forwards and center.

Sometimes you easily can make this defense a 2-3 zone simply by dropping your post player to the baseline area. This decision is predicated on the opponent's ability or inability to attack the middle of the defense based on their personnel. But, as a good rule of thumb, if no trapping is involved, the 2-1-2

zone should remain in that form regardless of where the basketball goes.

DIAGRAM 7: Extended 2-1-2 Defense. If your team is blessed with decent size, extend the 2-1-2 a bit or even meet the ball as the goal is covered by larger players.

DIAGRAM 8: 2-1-2 Chase. If you have a pair of quick players on the perimeter, chase the ball, have your low people cover the wings and leave your big man in the middle.

DIAGRAM 9: 22 Defense. The 22 is a 2-1-2 extended to the half-court line. It's a scramble defense as there are few rules and a lot of chances are taken. One rule is that once the ball crosses the half-court line, the defenders are moving. X5 always has basket coverage, so most of your damage is done with four players.

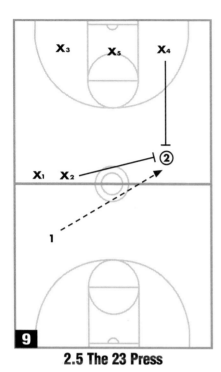

9

2.5 The 23 Press

The 23 press is a 3/4-quarter court press. Personnel-wise, keep the quick

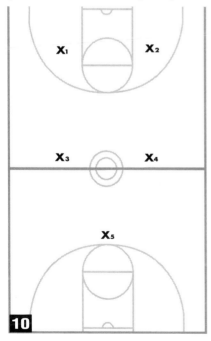

10

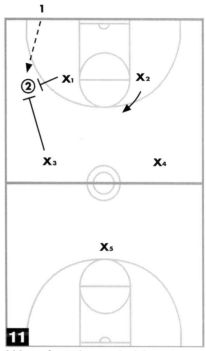

11

kids up front close to the inbounder.

DIAGRAM 10: The 23 Press. X3 and X4 are the forwards and one is the communicator. Put your best defensive anticipator (most teams have one) in the second row as a lot of lob passes come this way. X5 is a goalkeeper, usually the center. To start this press, allow the first pass. Many times, this press is token in nature just to give the offense a different look or add a little pressure. If you holler "23, 5" the players know it's a 2-2-1, 3/4-court press to start and man-to-man in the half-court defense. Also, tell 5 to stay home unless there is an opportunity for a lob-pass interception. If 5 gets itchy fingers, well-coaches teams are going to score behind him.

DIAGRAM 11: The 23 Press — Initial Motion. When 1 inbounds to 2, X1 and X3 greet 2 with a trap. X2 rotates back toward the middle of the court.

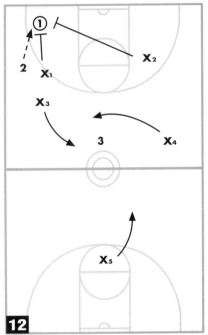

12

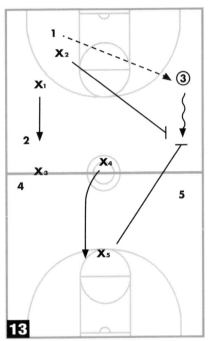

13

DIAGRAM 12: The 23 Press – Moving The Offense Backward. O2 has the ball and most likely has dribbled the ball. With a trap upon him, 2 looks to get the ball back to 1, who, if he's doing his job, is staying behind the initial trap. When the pass goes back to 1, X1 and X2 trap him. X3 rotates back toward the center of the court. X4 sprints to cover the open player (3). If the offense does get to the 10-second line, our defense falls back into an even-front 21 (2-1-2 zone defense).

DIAGRAM 13: The 23 Press — Final Rotations. 3 makes his move to get open. 1 passes to 3. 3 dribbles (most likely) and meets another trap, created by X5 who has moved into the backcourt and X2 who has rotated back from his trap of 1. X4 sprints back to cover the goal. X3 now is covering 4 and X1 covers the potential moves of 2.

2.6 The 1-3-1 Zone

When centering your defensive system around man-to-man defense, which is aided by an even-front zone, you need to add an odd-front zone to your defensive arsenal. By nature, a 1-3-1 (31 defense) zone is a half-court trap in waiting. Against teams featuring a strong perimeter game, this defensive gem is especially effective.

14

DIAGRAM 14: The 1-3-1 Zone. In the 1-3-1 defense, X1 is a quick guard or can be a quick forward who can stop the dribble. X1 sets the tone of the defense and if quick enough, X1 meets the dribbler just as he crosses the 10-second line. X2 and X3 generally are an off-guard and quick forward, respectively. If you have a couple of kids with a long wingspan, these two spots are the perfect positions for them. X5 is the center with the job of being as big as possible at all times. X4 has a tougher job. He needs to possess decent lateral movement and anticipate well (try to put a smart kid here).

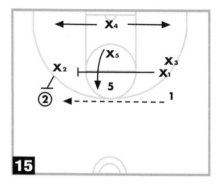

15

DIAGRAM 15: 1-3-1 Zone — Initial Movement. 1 is met by X1 and dribbles to his right. If 1 passes to 2, X1 and X2 trap 2. X5 jumps in front of 5. X4 remains alert on the baseline for what may come next.

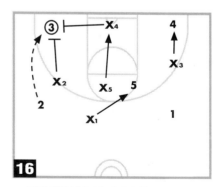

16

DIAGRAM 16: 1-3-1 Zone —

Continued. If 2 looks to the baseline and passes to 3, X4 shifts to that side and X2 drops down to create a trap. The opposite wing defender (X3) always drops down to cover an opposite corner pass. X5 drops into the lane and X1 rotates back to the top of the key.

2.7 Extending The Zone Into A Press

After confusing teams with a half-court 1-3-1 defense, extend the zone and make it into a press. The 33 defense is a 1-2-1-1, 3/4-quarter press. The 33 often is a token and is applied if a team takes a time-out to adjust to an earlier pressure look. The 33 allows an inbound pass.

The 34 defense also is a 1-2-1-1 but is a full-court press. It's successful if you've already employed other pressure defenses early in the game (i.e. the 54 defense or the 23 defense). The 54 and 23 allow an inbound pass, then trap. The

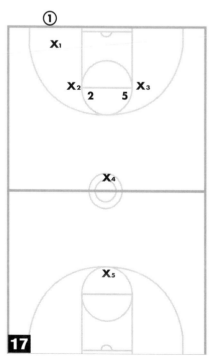

17

34 swarms the basketball at all time.

DIAGRAM 17: The 1-2-1-1 Press Set-Up. X1's responsibility is of the utmost importance in this type of press. Ideally, X1 is an agile post player. X1 raises his hands three-quarters of the way up so when 1 throws his inbound pass, X1 extends and possibly can deflect the pass, which X2 or X3 can recover and score easily. X2 is a quick guard and smart anticipator. X3 is the same type of player as X2. X4 needs to have some range as he's a linebacker-type player — roving, anticipating and communicating. X5 usually (not always) is the center.

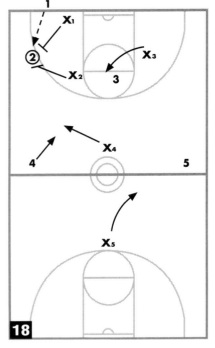

DIAGRAM 18: The 1-2-1-1- Press In Action. 2 receives the inbound pass from 1. X1 and X2 immediately trap 2. X3 fronts 3. X4 fronts 4. X5 rotates to thwart a lob pass to 5, remembering his main duty is to guard the goal.

For a breakdown of all of the defenses mentioned in the previous sections, refer to the following form below (Form 1, below).

2.8 Zone Offense

On the offensive end, when the defense sets up in a zone, it's either going to be an even-front (2-1-2 or 2-3) or an odd-front zone (1-2-2 or 1-3-1). Consider 3-2 zones as modified 1-2-2 zones and attack them accordingly.

DIAGRAM 19: Attacking A 2-1-2 Zone. Against a 2-1-2, go with a 1-3-1 zone offense. Give even-front zone teams a standard approach, playing off the reasoning that you can lull them into thinking they know what's coming. Then, add in an alteration or two and it should lead to a score. 1 dribble penetrates and looks to pass to either 2 or 3, who both are your best perimeter shooters. 4 constantly moves along the baseline, staying on the opposite side of the ball and moving

Complete Defensive Nomenclature

5 – Man-to-man in the half-court

52 – Picking up at the 10-second line out of man defense

53 – Three-quarter court man-to-man pressure

54 – Full-court man-to-man run-and-jump press

21 – A 2-1-2 half-court zone

22 – A scramble press out of 2-1-2

23 – A 2-2-1, three-quarter zone press

24 – Does not exist in system

31 – A 1-3-1- half-court zone defense

32 – Trapping out of a 1-3-1 zone

33 – A three-quarter court, 1-2-1-1 zone press

34 – A full-court, 1-2-1-1 zone press

1

accordingly. 5 is the post block and should be instructed to move just off the block on each side of the lane, back and forth, to be a visible target for teammates to spot. If 5 can shoot a free throw, you're in business. With proper ball movement, 5 may be able to get deeper into the zone than originally anticipated.

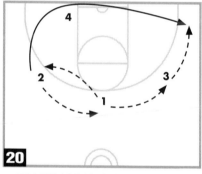

DIAGRAM 20: Wing-Cut Vs. Even-Front Zone. 2 receives a pass from 1. 2 returns the pass to 1 and cuts off an automatic screen set by 4. Most times 2 can maneuver for the opening on the other side of the floor. The wing-cut is an effective zone offensive move, especially for the hot shooter. Call out the shooter's uniform number, which signals this player is about to become the cutter. This series is a solid one when a last shot is needed.

When attacking an odd-front zone defense, it's a fallacy that you must use an even-front offense. There's a nifty 1-2-2 offense that does a good job when attacking a typical 1-3-1 zone defense.

DIAGRAM 21: Odd-Front Offense Vs. Odd-Front Defense. Put the best shooters on the low block to start the set. This set is a continuity pattern, of sorts, but also can be used as a non-rotating, stationary 1-2-2 offense. The offense starts with 1 dribbling to one side (in this example, to the left). 2 makes a jab step toward the basket, then out to receive a pass from 1.

DIAGRAM 22: Movement Against Odd-Front Defense. After receiving the pass, 2 might be open for a shot. If not, 4 drops down the lane, looking for a pass from 2. 5 comes across the lane, also looking for a pass from 2. 3 hesitates momentarily, then comes up the lane looking for a shot. If

2 can't find any of those shooters, then 2 passes back to 1 and goes through the lane replacing 3.

A coaching tip is to instruct 1 to look for shooting opportunities once the defense becomes comfortable with the rotation of the offense. With the defense thinking about all of the rotation possibilities, 1 might be able to get an open look without too much effort.

Like all zone offenses, finding seams in the defense is vital to success. Instruct your players to run two versions of the 1-2-2 offense against odd-front zones. Our previous diagrams detailed the 1-2-2 rotate but a 1-2-2 regular also is effective.

block and reverse it to a free shooter. The set starts with one shooter on the block (3) and one shooter in the back-court (2). Dribble penetration and ball reversal are crucial to the success of this offense.

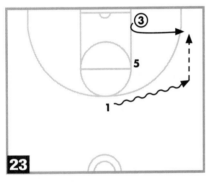

DIAGRAM 23: 1-2-2 Regular Zone Offense. 1 dribbles wide and passes to 3 who has popped out to the corner. 5 drops down to the low post. This change works because defenses start cheating toward cuts they've already seen. Changing the cutting pattern often leads to a quick hoop.

This is the same thinking used when switching to a 2-1-2 regular offensive set or a 2-1-2 rotating offensive set, which typically are run against a standard 1-2-2 defense or a jug zone.

DIAGRAM 24: 2-1-2 Regular Offense Vs. 1-2-2 Defense. In this regular set, look to get the ball to the low

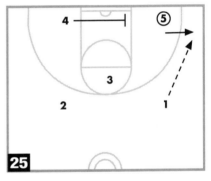

DIAGRAM 25: 2-1-2 Rotating Offense Vs. 1-2-2 Defense. The post players (4 and 5) start on the blocks. 1 passes the ball to the corner, this time to 5, on the baseline. 4 cuts to the mid-

Half-Court Man-To-Man Offensive Rules.

1. Concentrate on spacing — players need to be 15-18 feet apart in half-court set.
2. Non-point people need to look to the point guard for direction.
3. Point guard always is in contact with the bench, especially in dead-ball situations.
4. Once the play is called, others repeat the name or signal it.
5. Point guard needs to let the play gel or solidify before running it.
6. Players near the lane area need to avoid a three-second call.
7. Non-guards — it is tough to pass off the dribble.
8. Avoid skip passes vs. man-to-man defense.
9. Big people — keep dribbling to a minimum.
10. When the shot is taken, non-shooters holler "SHOT!" to aid teammates who may be out of position.

2

Half-Court Zone Offensive Rules

1. Advance the ball with the pass.
2. Shots come from dribble penetration from point guard.
3. Always be on the lookout to reverse the ball versus this type of defense.
4. Ball fakes are a must from all five players.
5. Shot fake-ball fake is a good combination of skills versus zones of any variety.
6. Against traps, one guard stays behind the double-team.
7. Post people need to come as high as they can to aid troubled teammates.
8. Skip passes or cross-court passes are allowed in zone offensive set.
9. Two-hand passes are a must.
10. Bounce passes work well in some sets.

3

dle. If 5 can't get a pass to 4, then players rotate the back triangle.

DIAGRAM 26: Rotation Of Back Triangle. 5 passes back 1, then goes to the foul line. 3 replaces 4, who has made the baseline flash move and the offense is ready to attack again.

The combination of regular and rotating sets out of the 1-2-2 and the 2-1-2 gives ample scoring opportunities to teams patient enough to work on them until they not only know the offenses but also know the many options the offenses provide. Dummy all of your offenses at the end of each practice and do it without defense.

Now that the entire offensive picture

is in place, you have something to play against when facing man-to-man (from Chapter 1) or zone defenses. To recap, review the above two forms (Forms 2 and 3) and be sure these rules are ingrained in your players' heads.

2.9 Preseason Review

When evaluating how ready your team is to start the season, there are a number of factors to consider.

Factor No. 1 — Did you pick the right team? Nothing frustrates a high school coach more than coming out of the preseason gate a little thin talent-wise. Here's what to do.

Keep a watchful eye on the younger kids — namely the ninth-grade and junior varsity team — always keep an open mind regarding roster changes. Some athletic directors prefer to see the final rosters drawn in blood but injuries or poor play dominate how you assemble your roster. Granted, it is easier to move kids up than to send them down but sometimes a coach has to make a bold move to stir things up. Tell your players that tryouts never end and no player should feel secure enough in his or her status to fail to demonstrate the necessary energy required for success.

Factor No. 2 — Are people out of position? Sometimes, a tune-up is all your program lacks. Talk to your coaching staff. Players out of position is a common early-season dilemma. Back-court problems top a long list of concerns entering the season. Perhaps your best team leader and ball-handler is a forward. Make the switch. You will never regret having a tall guard.

Factor No. 3 — Are you allowing time for preseason injuries to heal? Ankle woes and shin splints top most coaches' lists when it comes to nagging preseason injuries. Rest is the only cure for these two physical problems. The tendency to over-tape and play prematurely has kept a simple ankle hurting for a lot longer than it should. Kids who try to play through shin pain end up out of the lineup for a lot longer period of time than necessary. Rest early. Play more later. It's a simple formula to follow.

Factor No. 4 — Are your coaching roles clearly defined? Be sure your coaches know their roles and what's expected of them in practice and in games. Plus, players need to focus on playing and never should be confused by coaching mix-ups. Assign duties early on (Form 4 below). Here is a good breakdown of responsibilities for assistant varsity, junior varsity and ninth grade coaches.

Factor No. 5 — Tighten the discipline belt. Often times preseason work is so vital that coaches let their guard

---

Job Description For Coaches

*__Assistant Varsity Coach__ – The assistant coach has no true leadership role on the team other than to aid the varsity coach. From a hierarchy standpoint, however, he or she must be considered second in command to the head coach. Duties include attending all team functions, including each and every practice. The head coach may want the varsity assistant coach to set up practice, tape ankles and other related duties. Most years this coach is a sounding board for the head coach. He or she may be in charge of duties such as scouting, personnel evaluation or film.

*__Junior Varsity Coach__ – The JV coach's primary responsibility is to make a mini-varsity of his or her team. He or she must be willing to demonstrate complete loyalty to the head coach by running the varsity coach's entire system. Top job for the JV coach is two-fold. First, he or she must play each member of the team each and every game without exception. Secondly, he or she must teach and play man-to-man defense in all situations. Variations from these two guidelines will not be tolerated. The JV coach should attend all varsity practices. He or she also may be asked to scout and view film.

*__Ninth Grade Coach__ – The ninth grade coach's system also should mirror the varsity. Top job is to run at least a skeletal version of the varsity offensive system. Man-to-man defense should be instructed and played at all times. No excuses will be tolerated for deviations from this guideline. The ninth grade coach may be asked to scout, view film and compile stats.

4

Proper Player's & Coach's Diet

Breakfast

Cereal, fruit & milk

Provides carbohydrates & protein

Mid-morning snack

Fruits, bagels, granola bars or yogurt

Keeps minds sharp & bodies energized

Lunch

Sandwich, fruit, carrot sticks

Helps avoid mid-afternoon drowsiness

Afternoon snack

Peanut butter sandwiches, cheese and
     crackers, yogurt or fruit

Maintain energy to promote peak
     performance

Dinner

Lean meat, vegetables, starch and low-fat milk

Replenishes carbohydrates; provides protein for rebuilding and repairing tissues; and prepares body for another day's recycle

Note: Sugary snacks are tempting but provide very little vitamins and minerals. Carbohydrates are a must while being active in strenuous workouts. One-hundred percent fruit juices are handy in providing the carbs needed and the much-needed fluids. Also, athletes should have a drink about every 15 minutes during a strenuous workout.

Note: The essential difference between a player's diet and a coach's diet is that coaches need more protein on game day and they need to hydrate less during practices and games. Coaches and players need to refrain from the use of junk food, i.e. potato chips, sugar drinks (such as soda pop) and candy.

5

being on time and proper attitude. Teaching is important at this time of year but a loose ship struggles to stay afloat for four months. Tighten your belts now. If you don't, all the time you're spending on instruction won't be worth anything. It doesn't take make to unravel all of your hard work.

Factor No. 6 – Slow down. Take this time to evaluate your own agenda. Are you running at a break-neck speed? If so, slow down. In a short preseason, sometimes coaches not only push their kids but they also push themselves, sometimes to the point of harm. Self-evaluation of key areas such as rest and diet is beneficial to the coach as well as the team. Form 5 to to the left shows what players and coaches should be eating.

2.10 Creating A Deeper Team

One of the most difficult jobs for any coach is keeping the troops happy. Set up practices to allow non-starters the opportunity to take a job away from a starter. Every night is an open tryout. There always are those kids who are ahead of the so-called pack but even those players can't be given too much of a comfort zone. Keep the door open for change. Shutting the door the first night puts players at risk of assuming a secondary role on your squad. You never want that.

Plus, varsity coaches should try to have at least a nine- or 10-player rotation every game. Think about it. If you are a coach who likes to press, then you should be playing that many kids. If you favor a run-and-jump style of defense in the full-court, all 12 of your kids should play. If you walk the ball up the court, then you need to have back-ups for key positions such as point guard, center and either shooting

down when it comes to rudimentary discipline areas such as haircuts, dress and personal habits such as shaving,

guard or shooting forward. This gives you at least an eight-player rotation. The point is that playing more people keeps starters fresh. Nobody likes mop-up time and if you subscribe to that style of coaching basketball, then you're opening up your team for problems as the season progresses.

But, many coaches aren't sure how to get role players key minutes. There's no better way to develop a bench than to stick an inexperienced player in a game early with an experienced bunch. You'll be surprised how well this so-called role player adapts to his or her new surroundings. There's nothing greater than seeing a freshman score off a great pass that an upperclassman threw right on the money in the open court. By continually keeping kids continually with players of the same skill level, you reinforce a negativity that may cause a lot of confidence problems. Surprise an unsuspecting sophomore or two in key games by thrusting them into the lineup at crunch time. A test of fire is far better than working hard in practice versus the older kids because — let's face it — practice is still practice.

2.11 The "Christmas Classics"

Christmas tournaments are all the rage these days as athletic directors seek to put a few more dollars in the athletic coffers and coaches seek another mechanism for expanding their bench placating a malcontent or two with more playing time. My personal beef with the holiday stuff is what it does to the family unit.

Back in the good old days, most states gave kids a healthy Christmas break. I used to give my players an entire week off and scheduling was done with that break in mind.

Unfortunately, those days are long gone, and now from the time basketball rosters are selected until the gun goes off in the final postseason game, kids have very little time to themselves. Plus, players deserve family time and a chance to enjoy the holidays.

View the Christmas break as a teaching time. Most years a few games have been played up to this point in December and with the break the prudent coach is given the chance to clean up trouble spots. There are three main trouble spots that can be addressed without the pressure of moving December's regular-season games right into a Holiday Classic match-up.

Trouble Spot No. 1 — Trouble at point guard. A lot of coaches automatically think their team's point guard should be the player who comes out for the squad to play guard. If you automatically hand the basketball to a smaller player, who, because of his or her size, or lack of it, and expect them to run your team with great precision, then you may be making a big mistake. But, it's not too late to rectify your error.

Point-guard problems manifest themselves versus full-court pressure. Nothing thwarts your team's chances for success than turnovers against presses. True point people welcome pressure by the defense because they love to attack. Never be afraid to put your team's leader in this valuable position. Put defensive pressure on every player you have, then see who does the best job of advancing the ball without error.

Trouble Spot No. 2 — Too many missed free throws. Coaches whose teams don't make enough free throws inevitably don't spend the necessary time in practice on free-throw shooting. You should shoot two sets of foul shots during each two-hour practice. Shoot the first batch following extensive pre-game warm-up drills so that players are somewhat winded. Have players shoot and chart 25 attempts. At the end of a full-court scrimmage, which usually occurs at the end of practice, or even at the end of half-court work, shoot another round of 25. The key to success is when foul shots are shot in games, there are very few, if any, times that players move to the foul line rested.

Trouble Spot No. 3 — Are you playing the right people? Team chemistry is the most nebulous of variables when it comes to finding the ideal five or six kids to maintain starting positions. Have a solid sixth man, who often is better than the other five players, to provide a life when he or she enters the game.

December's break is also a good time to find out who is doing what. The charts you keep don't lie and neither do the shooting statistics. Remember, who to play or not to play ranks right up there as one of the most difficult decisions you make that can affect your season's outcome. For now, it's still plenty early enough to mix and match player combinations in practice. You might be surprised by the results.

2.12 New Year's Resolutions

Like most people, basketball coaches need to look within themselves and make New Year's resolutions, which can improve their job performance and how they view the world in general. Take a look at the following possible New Year's resolutions.

Resolution No. 1 — Ditch the scapegoat theory. An unbecoming coaching technique is to assess blame to someone or something that had no effect on the outcome of the games,

especially after losses. Special targets for this abuse are referees. Losing coaches who blame game officials for their losses pass on a dangerous message to their troops and one that can be carried over into the real world. Having a scapegoat is dangerous because it keeps the team from addressing the real reasons for defeat.

Resolution No. 2 — Practice less as the season progresses. Let up on your players as the season progresses, thereby making practices crisper, shorter and more fun as the postseason approaches. Preseason work and regular-season practice until mid-January require conditioning, teaching and team unity time. As the season moves along, coaches need to back off a bit, giving their players the opportunity to save their strength for games. Player burnout occurs if coaches drive their teams too hard.

Resolution No. 3 — Make sure the kids are having fun. Adding contests such as knock-out or 21 to a coach's practice repertoire goes a long way in making the day-to-day grind of coaching more enjoyable. You might be surprised that the smallest of prizes can aid bragging rights to a particular skill event and the players get to see the coach in a different light, especially if he or she participates in the skills event.

Resolution No. 4 – Vow to give assistants more responsibility. Guidelines for responsibilities and duties are established early (see Form 4 in this chapter). But the thoughtful, caring coach makes each assistant feeling like he or she is part of the team.

Resolution No. 5 — Cleaning up the table. Proper game management and efficiency comes from cleaning up the scorer's table. Make certain the

Proper Time-Out Management

Follow these rules during a 30-second time-out:

1. Player remain on the floor.
2. When time-out is given, non-players get water from the manager to give the players.
3. No one speaks except the coach.
4. Remaining players huddle in a circle around the team.
5. Eye contact with the head coach.
6. No griping.
7. No fussing.
8. Strict attention.
9. Break as a unit.
10. Non-player or manager wipes the floor area clean before players return to the floor and bench.

Follow these rules during a full time-out:

1. Players coming off the floor sit.
2. Others huddle around the coach.
3. Coach may consult with team members, assistant coaches or speak himself.
4. Anyone not being spoken to needs to be quiet.
5. Coach talks to players seated in front of him or her.
6. No other talking.
7. Water already should be provided.
8. Time-outs are short – use them wisely.
9. Huddle together before returning to the floor.

6

scorer's table is up to snuff and that adults hold the key jobs. Coaches and scorers should follow the International Association of Approved Basketball Officials, Inc. set of instructions.

Resolution No. 6 — Cleaning up the wardrobe issue. We've let our guard down in the area of game apparel for coaches. Gone are the days when coaches dressed to kill for their games. There's nothing wrong with gentlemen and ladies wearing their "Sunday Best"

clothes for basketball games.

Resolution No. 7 — Cleaning up poor media habits. Coaches owe it to their players to nurture and develop a good relationship with the media. Failing to call in scores, failing to list top scorers and rebounders, etc., rob kids of the opportunity to shine publicly. This game is not about coaches. The limited opportunity players have, time-wise, to excel in the gym should never be underestimated by coaches.

Resolution No. 8 — Time-out use. Coaches never find the time (no pun intended) to instruct their team in the proper use of a time-outs. Players and coaches should practice 30-second and full time-outs in practice, scrimmages and exhibition games before the season begins. Form 6 shows what should happen during time-outs.

Sample December Practice Plan

Varsity Boys Basketball Practice Plan (2 hours)

5:00-5:05	Stretch
5:05-5:10	Free shoot
5:10-5:15	10 laps around the gym
5:15-5:25	Pre-game, zig-zag and timed drills
5:25-5:45	Half-court scrimmaging (review end game)
5:45-6:00	50 free throws (water break)
6:00-6:15	Work on 54 press versus seven defenders
6:15-6:30	Full-court scrimmage work with 54 and 34 presses
6:30-6:40	Special situations
6:40-6:50	Half-court trap offenses
6:50-7:00	Sprints, laps, free-throw drills (if time)
	End of practice

7

Chapter 3

JANUARY: THE BUSIEST MONTH OF THE YEAR

January is a critical month for the success of your team. It also is the busiest month of the year. Scheduling woes often force the athletic director to place most games in January. January also is the time to address key issues for your team.

3.1 How To Win Close Games

It's important to be a stickler for detail and leave nothing to chance. One area of concentration that deserves a lot of practice time is implementing a philosophy on how to handle the close game. The following is a list of variables to aid you in putting together a sound offensive and defensive philosophy for close games. Blowouts aren't much fun and the challenges inherent in tight games help teams and coaches grow.

Variable No. 1 — Practice what you might see. If you're not a fan of using the game clock in practice – become one. Experiment with different late-game situations. Put 30 seconds on the clock and have your starters be behind by 3 or 4 points. Have one of your assistants coach the reserves, then coach your team the way you would in a real game under adverse circumstances. Take time-outs to explain strategy. Press if you need to and get your team into the habit of not only paying attention to you but also paying attention to the clock.

Variable No. 2 — Understanding protecting a lead. It's frustrating to see a team play so well for most of the game, only to blow it at the end by making mistake after mistake. There should be no surprises for players by game time. I cringe at coaches' post-game quotes such as "We weren't ready for their press," or "We didn't expect that defense at the end." Most coaches have a point in the game when their teams are ahead when they can pull the reins back a bit and slow things down. Without a shot clock to dictate tempo, the high school coach has an advantage over his college and professional counterparts. Start protecting leads of 6 points or more around

> **["Blowouts aren't much fun and the challenges inherent in tight games help teams and coaches grow."]**

Freeze Mode

Each coach needs to establish the time of game when to instruct the offense to be in a freeze mode.

1. Start the freeze mode with 4 minutes or less left in the fourth period.
2. Your lead should be at least 6 points (if you're comfortable with that number).
3. Continue to run your offense while being more selective. Use clock and get good shots in the paint.
4. Instruct players that getting out of freeze mode by taking a poor shot results in their removal from the game.
5. This is not a stall. It's patience with an offensive set.
6. Work on freeze mode every day in practice.

1

Deep-freeze mode

Patience and discipline are keys to running a successful deep freeze in the half-court. The deep freeze begins around the 2- or 2 1/2-minute mark and again you should be up 6 points but could be up 4.

1. Instruct players that the only acceptable shots are lay-ups and the subsequent fouls that may result.
2. If the defense is in zone, move the offense out near the 10-second (half-court) line and attempt to force the opponent to play man-to-man.
3. This is not a keep-away or monkey-in-the-middle philosophy. Players still should attack the basket if the opportunity presents itself.
4. Get an extra ball-handler or two on the floor to minimize turnovers. Nothing changes the course of the end-game situation than missed lay-ups, missed free throws or turnovers.
5. When running the deep freeze in practice, add a sixth or seventh defender to force your offense to think. The ball must end up in the right person's (or people's if you have several solid ball-handlers) hands.

2

the 4-minute mark.

Variable No. 3 — Freeze versus deep freeze. Check out the two forms on this page to see the differences between a freeze mode and a deep-freeze mode.

Variable No. 4 — The importance of free throws. It bears repeating — shoot two groups of 25 foul shots during most practices and if time allows — shoot more. Never underestimate the significance of foul shots and never short-change your team's chances for end-game success by not practicing this important shot (Form 3, next page).

Variable No. 5 — Improve techniques by watching other games. Pay close attention to special situations when watching games on television. See how other coaches run clock. Watch how they determine the time of the game they slow the ball down. Watch others implement their own freeze and deep-freeze patterns. Every coach is different and every coach has something to offer.

3.2 Making January Practices Better

Although there is room for improvement in most practice settings, as the season approaches the halfway point, which for most schools is January, the thoughtful coach looks for ways to make the practice setting better for all participants.

By January, it's time to shorten practices a bit. In preseason and even as the

Free-throw practice methods

These methods not only enhance free-throw competition in practice but also improve results.

1. Never shoot practice free throws when the team is rested.
2. Always run your free-throw drills after scrimmaging or after running drills.
3. To enhance a shooter's free-throw style and routine, always instruct each shooter to shoot 25 consecutive shots, then move to the next shooter.
4. Enhance free-throw competition by interrupting all shooters from time to time and set the stage as if you're in a game. Blow the whistle and tell the team they're down two with one second left. Tell them the next two shots are a one-and-one and they need both to go to overtime.
5. It is difficult to simulate actual game conditions for practice rounds of free-throw instruction. Tapes of crowd noise may be put on the public address system. Single out individuals at the end of practice and put them in end-game situations such as previously mentioned.
6. Free-throw games are a good tool. Put a can of soda at half-court for the winner of that day's competition or drills. Kids like not only team competition but individual competition as well. **3**

season progresses to Christmas, request a two-hour time slot for practice. But, by January, players should be in shape and the best way to keep them fresh (in such a tough month like January) is to reduce the time they're in the gym. Knock a half-hour or so off practice at this time.

At the same time, shorten drills and station work. This should be reduced to 10 minutes or less at this point in the season. Stress concentrating on the goal at hand and move on. Remember, these players still are growing physically and their bodies need a chance to recover, so back off running a drill for 30 straight minutes.

Shortening the practice day also entails less full-court work and more half-court work. Sure, players prefer to scrimmage every minute of every practice but to minimize injury and to save their legs, refrain from too much full-court work, which means more focus on the half-court. In fact, bring the scrimmage to the half-court. This improves man-to-man defense and helps players on both sides of the ball pick up the nuances of your half-court offense.

Along with backing off the physical demands of players at practice, back off the talking as well. You can keep everyone on the same page without boring them to death. If you want to lecture, take the kids into a classroom. By January, the players have heard everything you want to say.

3.3 Mid-Season Personnel Evaluation

January is a good time of year to evaluate personnel and make decisions to affect the remainder of the regular season through the postseason. Begin with a careful inspection of player statistics (examples on following pages).

By now, you have a good handle on your starting five, your substitute pattern and the junior varsity's role in assuring that sub-varsity players are getting the time and the instruction they need to aid the team into the future.

Mid-Season Personnel Evaluation - Guards

Name	Points Per Game	Assists Per Game	Steals Per Game	Turnovers
Jack Flagg	9 ppg	4	1.8	27

Coach's Comments:

Jack is spending too much time passing off his dribble, a skill he's yet to master

4

Mid-Season Personnel Evaluation - Forwards

Name	Points Per Game	Assists Per Game	Steals Per Game	Turnovers
Jason Strout	7 ppg	1	3	54

Coach's Comments:

Jason may be our hardest worker yet. We love this kid!

5

Mid-Season Personnel Evaluation - Centers

Name	Points Per Game	Assists Per Game	Steals Per Game	Turnovers
Peter Sills	10 ppg	1	0.9	16

Coach's Comments:

Peter is the perfect post player for us in so many ways.

6

Mid-point also is a good time to reevaluate your thinking at both ends of the floor if things haven't gone all that well. Sometimes, all it takes is a small adjustment to right the ship. For instance, say you have a JV player who is starting to light it up, maybe he or she becomes a role player, too, for the varsity team for the second half of the season. Kids generally are fearless when it comes to this type of move.

Or, perhaps you've been toying with a special defense in practice but you haven't employed it in a game. Be bold. That one change may spell the difference between success and failure in the second half of the season.

Head coaches also should sit their staff down and record feedback from them regarding the hoop proceedings to date. Failure to listen to your staff's opinions on the season to date really can hurt the process. You even might hear something you don't want about your own coaching, which, if accepted, also may prove to be the difference in the last nine or 10 games of the season. Form 7 on the following page shows a sample of a staff feedback sheet completed by an assistant.

Another hint is to get your kids to redo their goal cards or change some of what they told you in November (Chapter 1.8). Now, for example, the player in Chapter 1 who wanted to work on his left hand and become more of a contributor may write his individual-goal thoughts as: "Our sea-

["Perhaps you've been toying with a special defense in practice but haven't employed it in a game. Be bold."]

Staff Feedback Sheet

1. Comments on the season at the mid-point: *To date we've done well. We really need to tighten our belts defensively, especially in the third period. We seem to come out lax after the half.*

2. Areas of concern: *Foul trouble. We're committing a lot of silly fouls early in the game.*

3. Suggested lineup changes: *Steve Barnes need to get more playing time.*

4. Suggested changes on offense: *Our motion offense has been a bit too freelanced at times. We need to go back to basics, especially cross-picks on the baseline.*

5. Suggested changes on defense: *We should half-court trap more.*

6. Other comments: *We're doing well. We just need to tweak a few items.*

7

son is going quite well and I feel I have improved my dribble with my left hand. I have also become a contributor for the team, as I have moved up to sixth man." The player's team goals in the preseason were the win 13 games and make the postseason. Now, he may write, "Well, we are well on our way to winning 13 games and we are playing patient, team ball. I believe if we continue to play the way we are, we're tourney-bound in the top 4."

If you're a film coach, then the halfway point is as good a time as any to evaluate your team's performance at both ends of the floor (Form 8 and 9 on the next two pages). Kids need firsthand evidence of their errors. Film has no

personality and it does not lie. Errors are right there for viewing, pure and simple.

If you've done your job, there shouldn't be a great deal of second-half adjustments. Use the half-way point to evaluate personnel. If they need it, now is the time to get your kids on the right track again or to fine-tune a machine that already is working properly.

3.4 Keys To Preparing For The Postseason

As January wanes, February soon will be upon you and it is incumbent upon the head coach to begin preparing his or her team for tournament play. The prudent coach gives his or her team ample opportunity to prepare for

["Film has no personality and it does not lie. Errors are right there for viewing, pure and simple."]

Video Review Checklist

1. Overview of contests: _____

_____

_____

2. Highlights: _____

_____

_____

3. Lowlights: _____

_____

_____

4. Standout individual plays: _____

_____

_____

5. Standout team play: _____

_____

_____

6. Comments: _____

_____

_____

8

what lies ahead.

Spend a good deal of time during the season scouting the opposition with a special eye on the postseason. Scouting is more than watching. The key to good scouting is looking for offensive and defensive tendencies and finding holes in the armor of the opponent. The two forms (Forms 10 and 11) on pages 53-54 help in scouting an opposing player and an opposing team.

Scouting also comes in the form of film. Depending on where you coach, it may or may not be easy to acquire film from an opponent's opponent. The proliferation of cable-access television companies around the country makes the acquisition of game film less arduous. There may be a minimal expense to acquire the finished product but a couple of phone calls and a small fee are better than haggling with a colleague about tapes.

Another key to preparing for the postseason is dealing with a different type of schedule. In many areas, some teams have to play-off to make the tournament while others already have secured a bye. A play-in game keeps you on a normal game-day frame of mind for preparation. Play-in teams keep their normal practice routines.

[**"Another key to preparing for the postseason is dealing with a different type of schedule."**]

Video Review Checklist

Opponent: _____

Date: _____

Final Score: _____

Comments: _____

_____

_____

_____

_____

9

If you have a week or more before your first game, give your players a couple of days off following the last regular-season game. After that, go right to work for three or four days, then play an exhibition or closed scrimmage. Bring back former players to keep it a more controlled environment. But, be sure to bring in competent officials for the scrimmage as you don't want your players to develop bad fouling habits at this point.

[**"If you have a week or more before your first game, give your players a couple of days off..."**]

Player Scouting Form

Player: _____ Team: _____

Date: _____ Game Results: _____

1. Shot Charts:

2. Player strengths: _____

_____

3. Player weaknesses: _____

_____

4. Individual tendencies_____

_____

5. Comments: _____

_____

10

Coaches also need to buckle down on curfew enforcement at this point in the season. Players need to keep their homework in tact. Assistant coaches need to lighten the load of the head coach by helping him or her with film work, the scouting notes and the practice preparation.

3.5 A Good Time To Firm Up Weak Spots

January usually gives the coach some teaching time. In many school districts, exam week freezes out games but allows for practice time. The gym always provides player an outlet from

Opponent Scouting Form

Player: _____   Date: _____

Game Results: _____

1. Shot Charts:

Score by periods:

2. First player off the bench: _____

3. Team's primary offense: _____

4. Team's primary defense: _____

5. Team's secondary offense: _____

6. Team's secondary defense: _____

7. Tendencies: _____

8. Comments: _____

_____

11

the rigors of taking tests. Some nights, simply let them shoot around, them move to half-court pick-up games.

By this point in the season, it's important to address team issues that may hurt the chances for success if not addressed now. A few examples of continuing trouble spots include having

"Use six or seven players on the defensive end in practice when learning to break pressure."

trouble versus zones, foul trouble and having trouble breaking presses.

Trouble No. 1 — Still having trouble vs. zones. Having trouble with zones is a common problem for teams. Once coaches on your schedule get the word that your team can't score versus any zone defense, you need to right the ship immediately. Poor shooting could be the problem and spending more time shooting may help. But, if your club is shooting somewhere between 25-33% from the floor versus zones, then you need to address this problem. About this time of year it's a good idea to take a look at an underclassman on your junior varsity squad who may be lighting it up from downtown. The sophomore may be waiting for a call-up. There are times this young player can ignite your team to great things. The postseason is on the horizon…this kid may be just what the doctor ordered.

Another tried-and-true method for teams struggling from the perimeter against zones is to set a goal for your team relative to a point in the contest where your team attempts to pull the opponent out of the zone to force them to play man-to-man. Spread your offense when you're up 4-6 points. Some opponents move to man-to-man immediately, while others try to stand their ground. Either way, be sure to run something to try to score in these situations. Don't have your kids stand flat-footed and just pass the ball as this typically results in a turnover.

Trouble No. 2 — Foul trouble. Nothing hurts the possibility of success

more than getting deep into your bench early, especially in important contests. For example, say your team is having trouble guarding the opposing post player. Your chance for success diminishes considerably when your own center is spending a lot of time on the bench. Try to assign two or even three people to guard this particular offensive player. By spreading the fouls along the bench, you not only give the big post player a few different looks but you also keep your best defender in the game.

Overall, foul trouble usually is due to stupid fouls, in particular, reaching. In practice, it might not be a bad idea to have players defend with their hands behind their backs, so they concentrate on moving their feet.

Trouble No. 3 — Still having trouble breaking presses. If you can't break a press at this point in the season, rethink how you're attacking them. Most high school hoop teams have little to no trouble versus zone pressure once kids settle into a specific zone press offense and stay way from "dribblitis."

Use six or seven players on the defensive end in practice when learning to break pressure. This keeps almost all kids involved in this portion of practice, plus if your offense can master beating six or seven defenders, then an opponent's press with only five players seems simple.

This chapter ends with a sample practice plan (Form 12) for a typical January practice. Remember, by

January, your practices should be closer to 90 minutes in duration rather than two hours.

Sample January Practice Plan
Varsity Boys Basketball Practice Plan (1 1/2 hours)

4:45-5:00	Talk in the locker room about grades. Nip any issues in the bud at this point.
5:00-5:10	Shorten shooting and warm-up period. Kids are stretching early on their own.
5:10-5:20	Zig-Zag drill, 30-second shooting drill
5:20-5:25	7 laps
5:25-5:35	3-man weave and one-on-one games at all six baskets
5:35-5:45	25 free throws
5:45-6:00	New wrinkles in the half-court
6:00-6:25	Half-court scrimmage
6:25-6:30	Sprints

End of practice

12

Chapter 4

FEBRUARY: CHAMPIONSHIP SEASON APPROACHES

4.1 Down The Stretch They Come

Ever wonder why some coaches get their teams to peak at the right time every year? If you do, then you need to know a few important variables about practicing to peak. Teams that seem to run out of gas as the season wanes obviously are spending too much time in the gym. The first thing to go for overused players is the legs. As mentioned in the January chapter, you already should have backed off the longer practices and started using a crisper, 90-minute format.

There are other variables that need to be employed as your team makes its way to the proverbial finish line.

Variable No. 1 — Keep players out of harm's way. It's funny to hear coaches say how tough they are and how tough their players are because of the coaches' toughness. Remember, punitive drills can lead to player injuries.

A couple of years ago a coach told me he had just been fired. He couldn't imagine why and during the course of our conversation he mentioned running a lay-up drill that involved smacking airborne players in the stomach with padded sticks. He said this was a particular favorite among the team…and it probably cost him his job. Don't run a drill that involves any punishment. Never implement any practice drill that does not imitate an actual game situation. If a kid gets hurt in your gym, it better be in a basketball setting.

Variable No. 2 — Stress dietary improvement. It's difficult for coaches to supervise players in their day-to-day diets. But, let's face it, teenagers consume way too much junk food. February is the time of year for coaches to continue to stress proper dietary habits. Encourage your players (through their parents of course) to start getting water-enriched fruits back into their diets. Preach the avoidance of potato chips and other salty snack foods as quick fillers in a pinch. Sometimes the best a good coach can do is hand out diet charts and send them home with players with a polite note, encouraging

> **"Never implement any practice drill that does not imitate an actual game situation."**

all parties to be more prudent about you, as the coach, wish them to eat.

Variable No. 3 — Sleep issues. Kids are notoriously lousy sleepers. One of the reasons you should have a curfew during the season is to at least have a mechanism in place that gets the players home. Of course, at that point, it's out of your control. Stress players get eight hours of sleep per night when they're in training.

Variable No. 4 — Days off never hurt. This time of year, always try to give players a day off from practicing following a road game. That does not mean they get to skip school. Make sure all players (managers and staff included) are at school by the first bell after a road game. Then, make sure they leave school at the end of the day so they can get the rest they need.

4.2 In A Tourney Frame Of Mind (On The Court)

It's time to turn thought to the post-season. Getting into a tournament frame of mind and doing the things it takes to make your team tournament-ready are not variables that should be taken lightly.

If time allows, play a scrimmage or exhibition game to keep the troops fresh. A plus would be to play this game "on the road" to emulate going on the road for a tournament game. This game should feature some of the variables you may face in your first-round opponent. For example, if your team is facing a legitimate center in the playoffs, then you should look for someone who has a taller player to

afford you and your team the opportunity to work on playing this type of player. Also, bring in former players so you can control the action but be sure to hire certified board officials. Let them know you'll be stopping the action from time to time. Remember, if playoffs are featuring officiating teams of three, hire three officials. No matter what they say, officials react and respond differently when working in a team of three versus a team of two.

4.3 In A Tourney Frame Of Mind (Off The Court)

Do your best to minimize hoopla that accompanies a post-season tournament, especially the day of the big game. Keep it as low key as possible. Most celebrations occur the night before and that's fine. Tell your players that the normal curfew is in place and you expect them to honor their preseason commitment to you and the team.

Another concern is that tournament time often brings out the worst in families. Parents schedule family events around your games like it's just another chance to shop, visit with relatives or spend a few days at a resort skiing. This is not a time for a player to get lost in a vacation mentality. You travel as a team, play as a team, eat a post-game meal as a team, return home as a team, stay put during the post-season days and players sleep in their own beds.

If you're new to this profession, be ready to be inundated with parental requests to remove their children from the team bus for one reason or another.

[**"You travel as a team, play as a team, eat a post-game meal as a team, return home as a team..."**]

It's a good idea to have a written policy in place forbidding players to depart a team vehicle to join a parent. If you give in to this one request to ride with a parent, you start an avalanche of them. Put your foot down and tell your team that being part of a team means being together for team activities, like traveling to a tournament venue.

Another thing to do as a team is to view film of the opponent the night before the big game. You'd be sur-

---

Scouting: Winning Hoops Academy

Team: _____   Date: _____

Final Score: _____

1. Shot Charts:

2. Substitution pattern: _____

3. Offensive strengths: _____

4. Offensive weaknesses:_____

5. Defensive strengths: _____

6. Defensive weaknesses: _____

7. If playing WHA next week, you would (offense): _____

8. If playing WHA next week, you would (defense): _____

Comments: _____

_____

1

---

prised how smart your team is if given the chance to be and they even may find weaknesses in your upcoming opponent that you overlooked.

4.4 Changes To Enhance Post-Season Play

February is the month for coaches to take a long, hard look at how their teams are going to be perceived in the post-season. If you, as coach, were about to play your own team, what would be your chief concerns? A good way to figure this out is to get a coaching colleague (whose team you don't play) to attend an end-of-season game and scout your club. Don't find out when this coach is coming to scout your team, so you don't try to do something different. Have this coach send the scouting report to you in writing, then follow up with a phone call so the coach can explain how he or she would attempt to beat you. A sample scouting form (Form 1) precedes this page.

After talking with that coach, assess your team. Don't over-coach at this point no matter what. Many coaches make wholesale changes in their systems simply for the sake of making changes. A better idea is to add a new wrinkle or two to your game plan, like adding a set play or two versus a man-to-man defense, which you haven't shown to this point in the season. Another wrinkle is to devise a new out-of-bounds play or two. Don't touch things like your primary offense or zone offense. Let the other guy worry about you.

Defensively, teams who play us know our primary defense is always single coverage, man-to-man defense (Form 2). So, you may want to show a zone once in awhile. You may have better success showing junk or unex-

Post-Season Defensive Checklist

As you prepare for the most important game of the season, have your players concentrate on the following list to enhance practices and the game itself. Kids respond to lists and are challenged by the written word, especially if combined with the spoken word.

1. **Sloppy Play** — The biggest problem in the tournament is the adjustment to tight officiating relative to sloppy play. You need to move your feet and keep your hands in the correct position without reaching.

2. **Talk** — We're moving to bigger arenas now. Be sure to communicate with your teammates on screens, switches and where the ball is being advanced with the dribble.

3. **Zones & Pressure** — We need to minimize sloppiness and stupid fouls, so when we're in our zone, concentrate on not reaching and moving as a unit.

4. **Inbounds Defense** — Pay attention to the bench because we may switch between zone and man or vice versa based on what we see from the opposing bench relative to the type of play being called. Communicate with the bench and each other.

5. **End Of Game** — We've spent a lot of time in preparing how we do things defensively at the end of the game. Our FIVE (man-to-man) defense is what got us here and we'll stick with it.

6. **Don't Take Matters Into Your Own Hands** — Review your playbook about what we don't do on defense, especially poor decisions like running by a shooter for a steal. A mistake brings the opponent's crowd into the game.

2

Post-Season
Defensive Goals

1. **Keep The Opposition Under 50 Points** — 16 out of 18 times this year we held our opponents to less than 50 points. That was our goal in the regular season and it is our goal now.

2. **Stay Out Of Foul Trouble** — Maintain aggressiveness but be smart.

3. **Pick Up The Charge** — Know the difference between flopping on the floor to take a charge and stepping up to take contact. Always keep the defensive triangle, which enables you to move from a one-pass-away stance to a help-position stopping contact.

4. **Talk On Rebounding** — Don't just talk on offense or defense, talk when the shot goes up. Don't put your teammates in a precarious position by leaving them out to dry when a shot is launched. Scream "SHOT!" and continue to act as a unit.

5. **Pull For Each Other** — All of us, including coaches and player who are not in the game, must be talking, helping and demonstrating loudly what is transpiring out on the floor.

3

Tournament Game
Preparation Checklist

1. Curfew are strictly enforced.

2. Travel bus rules apply.

3. We arrive at the game together. We leave after the game together.

4. Preseason practice attitude/post-season preparation.

5. We dress up.

6. We sit together as a group upon arrival to the tournament site.

7. Move around the building by groups of three or four to avoid confrontation.

8. No verbal exchanges with opponents or their fans before, during and after the game.

9. Post-game activities also are team events. Caution your parents accordingly.

10. We encourage our fans' participation in all we do but we discourage their taking over and interrupting our pre-game and post-game prepa-

4

pected zones to your opponent early in the contest as the element of surprise works better at this stage of the game. Either way, don't abandon your primary defense. If it's a scrappy, hustling, man-to-man defense, stick with it. Kids get psyched up for the individual match-ups, especially if you're playing a dominant player.

Set some overall post-season defensive goals (Form 3) to keep your team motivated as well.

This isn't the time of year to change game philosophies either. If you don't like to press but you know the other team doesn't handle pressure well, don't force your team into a press. Don't do something you haven't worked on previously. To be prepared fully, put together a tournament game preparation checklist (Form 4) so your team knows what is expected of them.

This chapter ends with a sample practice plan for a typical February practice.

[**"This isn't the time of year to change game philosophies either."**]

Varsity Boys Basketball Practice Plan (1 1/2 hours)

8:00-8:15   All drills

8:15-8:25   25 free throws (water break included)

8:25-8:45   Half-court scrimmage versus zones

8:45-8:50   More water

8:50-9:00   Discuss potential tourney opponents and walk through their offensive and defensive sets

9:00-9:15   Cleaning up passing in 3-2 motion set. Cleaning up trouble spots in zone offense passing

9:15-9:30   Full-court scrimmage

9:30-9:40   Running drills

End of practice

5

MARCH: WRAPPING IT ALL UP

5.1 Time To Take A Break

March is a good time to start winding down from the recently completed busy season. Coaching is a notoriously stressful job and if you are a prudent coach, insert time-off days into your schedule, which aids you physically and emotionally. The combination of physical exercise and the return to a proper diet (yes, we all eat a lot of the wrong food from time to time during the season) go hand-in-hand in returning you to a normal routine. The following are some key personal areas that should be at the top of your list if you want to return to a normal routine (if there ever is one).

Personal Issue No. 1 — Sleep issues. Sleep loss and poor sleep habits are a big problem during the season for coaches. Personally, I wasn't a worrier about my program but I was a notorious night owl. My wife moves right into the spare bedroom during the winter months because she knows the bed becomes my office. Papers are scattered everywhere. Game plans, practice

plans and videotapes all take up residence once tryouts end.

March is the time to get back into a healthy eight-hour-per-night sleep routine. This not only aids personal health but it also helps unify a family whose patience may have been stretched to the limit during the season.

Personal Issue No. 2 — Dietary issues. March also is a good time of year to return to a better diet. Most coaches eat on the run during the hectic months of the season and the food choice is often of the snack variety. Returning to a three-meal-per-day routine is vital for physical health.

Personal Issue No. 3 — Exercise. Along with the poor eating habits during the season, exercise goes by the wayside. Weight gain is often a problem for coaches, especially during the regular season. A trip to the family doctor is not a far-fetched idea this time of year.

Personal Issue No. 4 — Return to family activities. Face it, you've missed some family activities during the basketball season. Kids do like to

> **"March is the time to get back into a healthy eight-hour-per-night sleep routine."**

Watching Games at Home

Opponent: _____

Date: _____

Final Score: _____

Special Plays:

End-game possibilities: _____

_____

_____

Notes: _____

_____

_____

1

go to your games but what they don't like is the time you spend away from home involved in the activities they can't participate or witness. A weekend away at this point in the year may do the trick. Never underestimate the importance of family.

5.2 Using The NCAA Tournament As A Clinic Tool

Try to tape as many NCAA games as you can during the NCAA tournament. There are a lot of qualified college coaches out there and having the opportunity to break down what you've seen by watching film can provide a useful clinic tool for only the price of a tape, and of course, your time.

When watching a tape of a game, don't watch it like a fan would. Treat it as game film of your next opponent (use Form 1), especially in regard to end-of-game situations. You never can learn too much in regard to end-game situations. Whether it's the time to hold the ball or not, or simply utilizing an effective press-breaker, every coach should try to pick up some ideas while studying these games.

Other areas to note include out-of-bounds plays, time-out utilization, press-breakers and press personnel alignments.

Most importantly, be sure to share

this information with your team in the form of chalk talks. Don't just preach it to them — show them. Ask your players to identify what each team is doing. Players like to provide input to the overall learning process. Don't be so dictatorial in your approach that you leave out some kid who eats, breathes and lives for this stuff.

Of course, some things you watch won't pertain to your team simply from a talent perspective. There are going to be those plays that you can't run because your team doesn't have the players to execute them. But, you might be able to alter slightly some things you see to fit your needs. If you are watching a team and you decide to use one of their plays, give them credit and name the play after them. It's a little more fun than the standard numbers and colors.

5.3 Beware The Pitfalls Of March

The season is over but the job of the head coach has just begun. Yes, not much time off. But, March can be an enjoyable month as it's a time for reflection and a time to prepare for next year.

Basketball Equipment Inventory						
Equipment	Number	Condition	# Needed	Number Lost	Date	Comments

2

Referee Rating Sheet

Ratings: Fair 1-4   Good 5-8   Excellent 9-10

Name	Confidence in Ability	Attitude/Manner Handling a Game	Appearance on Court	Physical Condition	Court Coverage & Signals

3

Putting the season to bed properly is an important aspect of your job. For example, getting back all of the team's equipment is a part of your job, not your manager's job. A strict inventory (Form 2, previous page) is critical to the success of this area and it generally should fall on the shoulders of the coaching staff. You and your assistants should perform the tedious task of collecting and keeping track of all equipment, including basketballs.

The only apparel items you should be issuing are practice jerseys. Kids are infamous for losing stuff. As for uniforms, keep them in a truck and clean them after every game. Always collect all school gear after the last game of the season and don't fall for the excuse that the stuff will be cleaned and delivered to your office after someone's mother does the laundry.

Medical kits and other sundry supplies need to be inventoried as well.

Game Film Inventory Sheet

Opponent	Date	Color Code/Other	Comment

4

Make a list of what medical supplies are needed for your summer program (if that falls under the auspices of the school) or for next season.

March also is a good time to address any staff concerns. As head coach, you are involved in some type of evaluation process with your co-coaches. If not, then request a sit-down with your athletic administrator to offer your input. For example, if you had a problem getting your junior varsity coach to run your defensive system, then your boss(es) need to know. Don't let a problem of this nature fester to the point of a verbal confrontation. If you need backing from the administration, ask for it.

Another responsibility in March is to evaluate game officials. Don't underestimate your role in this process. Rely on input from your staff but don't let players be a part of this process. Be professional in your rating of officials (Form 3, previous page). They are people and are very serious about their officiating careers. There are a few people out there who you don't like to see but your rating sheet affords you the opportunity to professionally and secretly evaluate the men and women who call your games.

Any formal rating you do along these lines should be private with copies of all correspondence made and locked away where no one can see what you and your coaches have done.

Don't forget to organize your recently completed season's game film (use Form 4). It is a much more arduous task to organize two or more seasons worth of film, tapes and DVDs than it is to tackle one season just after its completion.

Notice there is a section on the game-film inventory sheet designated for "color code/other." Color coding is an easy method to separate years. Pick a different color for each year. Of course, as you spend more time coaching, you'll need to reuse colors. At that point, use a dot or stripe along with the color to symbolize a different season.

One of the key aspects to organizing films, tapes and DVDs involves where to keep them. Use a bookshelf for easy access. Stashing film, tapes and DVDs away in a box becomes a cumbersome process, especially when you want to retrieve them. A bookshelf allows recorded games to be within your reach, whereas boxes cause you to seek and search, slowing down the entire process.

5.4 Prepare For The Summer

After you collect equipment, rate referees and catalog your game-film inventory, start planning for off-season camps and summer work. While expenses always are a factor in a player deciding on a camp, there are a number of team weekends or team camps that are priced reasonably. Get your kids together and make a list of things you'd like to do with them in the off-season. Check prices, then decide as a group what is fair to ask players to pay, then raise the difference. One good way to underwrite expenses is a team car wash. Also, check with your athletic director or booster club to see if the school or a supporting group plans to help.

If your team decides to play in an organized summer league, make certain every player who signs up for the league gets to play. There's no good reason for a coach not to play all of his or her kids in a summer hoop league game. These games don't count toward your regular season and there's no better way to turn kids off from hoops than to leave them on the bench in the off-season.

5.5 Smart Off-Season Decisions For Your Players

Stress injuries due to overuse are a major concern for players who take part in off-season basketball activities. The cautious, prudent player combines a period of rest with a steady diet of work. The key is to know when to back off and when it's safe to continue.

Rest always should come first. All basketball players need a break from the rigors of play. The day-to-day pounding on legs and feet takes a toll on all players. Tell your players a solid month of rest won't hurt them. Even during this month off, players can shoot alone or with a partner but they need to keep away from the pounding for a few weeks. Most high school players engage in 70-100 workouts per year during the regular season. Just imagine the wear and tear on their feet, ankles and shins.

If players have been diligent with allowing their bodies sufficient rest, they then move on to other activities. Strengthening exercises following a rest period are a good idea.

Every March, after a sufficient period of rest, contact your players and outline for them what you consider the areas to work in preparation for next season. These suggestions may include shooting drills, free throw drills or defensive work. Be sure the player is ready for off-season work and sometimes it's smart to include parents or

WHA
Winning Hoops Academy Boys Basketball

March 5, 2006

Dear Coach Jones,

Steve Barnes informs me that he has qualified and made your AAU team this summer.

You will enjoy Steve primarily because he is a hard worker.

Any time one of my players participates in a summer basketball event other than my own, I send along the attached form, which lists areas of skill development that I would appreciate you and your staff working with Steve on.

Please know that you can count on me for any follow-up. I would appreciate receiving a copy of your game schedule.

Steve is extremely excited about AAU and I know he will be a good addition to your team.

I am enclosing a self-addressed, stamped envelope so you may return a copy of the attached form to me for my records.

Sincerely,

Ron Brown

Head Coach

Winning Hoops Academy

5

guardians in these plans.

It is difficult to implement individual improvement skills for players as they so often are involved in AAU, team camps and summer leagues. March is a good time to start a conversation with AAU or YBOA coaches about encouraging them to concentrate on skills work with your players. Most AAU coaches are receptive to the needs of any participating players. A quick note or phone call solves a lot of problems and gives the other coach a clear indication of your concern for your player (see Form 5 and Form 6).

Now is the time to be thinking about keeping track of your players' work in the summer. If games are played, chart

Off-Season Skills Improvement Sheet

Player: _____

Skills needing work: _____

_____

_____

_____

Attitude: _____

_____

_____

_____

Comments: _____

_____

_____

_____

_____

6

them and your players' progress, just as you do during the regular season. AAU coaches will provide stats for you and as you move closer to the summer, you now realize this is a year-round job!

Chapter 6

APRIL: SPRING COACHING

6.1 Assessing Your Future Needs

A key coaching component for April is to find the time to take a realistic look at next season and to assess properly what it's going to take to improve your program. One of the most difficult

---

Player Position Needs Chart

1. Position _____

2. Specific Needs _____

_____

3. Incoming players' strengths _____

_____

4. Incoming players' weaknesses _____

_____

5. Players(s) who can fill the vacancy _____

_____

6. Incoming sophomore who may fill the vacancy _____

_____

7. Incoming freshmen who may fill the vacancy _____

_____

8. Do we need to adjust our system? _____

_____

9. Comments _____

_____

_____

1

Player Leadership Form

1. Type of leadership skills shown on the floor _____

_____

2. Type of leadership skills shown off the floor _____

_____

3. Academic strengths _____

_____

4. Academic weaknesses _____

_____

5. Ball-handling strengths _____

_____

6. Ball-handling weaknesses _____

_____

7. Shooting strengths _____

_____

8. Shooting weaknesses_____

_____

9. Attitude _____

_____

10. Comments _____

_____

_____

2

aspects of coaching high school kids is finding the right people to fit the positions needed to give the program continued success. Unlike college coaches, you don't have the luxury of recruiting to fill holes in the roster. Don't wait until November to start assessing your needs.

Compile a chart (Form 1, previous page) based on strengths, weaknesses and who can fill vacancies within your system.

The best place to start this evaluation process is to make a list of who is returning and who is leaving the team. For example, your senior post player is graduating in June. This big stud in the middle of the floor is almost impossible to replace. Unless you have a junior varsity player who can assume that position, you may be forced to alter your thinking offensively and defensively without this one player. If you have a good amount of quickness returning, you may want to consider more of a full-court style of defense.

Or, for example, it's your point guard who is graduating. A lot of kids think they can play this position but when push comes to shove — few can. The best bet is to find the best leader who can handle the ball and score. Use the form on the previous page (Form 2) to assess the leadership capabilities of a returning player.

After determining the leadership capabilities of several players, don't get stuck in the typical thinking that a point guard has to be a shorter guard-type. Never discourage a kid with a forward's body from wanting to run your team. Taller kids see over traps, they post up to create defensive mismatches and, if they shoot well, you're in business.

Of course, small guards are plentiful in a lot of hoop programs. Replacing a dandy point guard may be as simple as looking at your lower level teams.

6.2 What Do You Want To Add To Your Playbook?

Now is the time to get out your playbook and decide what you might want to add next season. Playbooks are one of the keys to your team understanding your offense, defense and spe-

---

Player Test Form

Name _____   Grade _____

Position _____

Essay: _____

In your own words, describe 4 of our inbounds plays: _____

_____

_____

_____

In your own words, discuss our 54 and our 34 press: _____

_____

_____

_____

3

---

cial-situation calls. At any time of year, test your players on the playbook (Form 3 previous page).

Remember the players who do a good job on your playbook tests. These could be the future leaders of your squad.

6.3 Improving Coach/Referee Relations

More should be done to promote better relations between coaches and officials. Far too many coaches in all sports treat the officials as the opposition and this philosophy rubs off on the players. Crowds follow suit and many times the result is ugly. Treat the officials how you would want to be treated — with respect.

Basketball referees work hard to hone their skills. They take pride in their craft and they aren't in the business of thinking they decide the outcome of the game. While some referees are better than others, the same can be said of coaches, players and athletic administrators.

To foster better relations between yourself and the officials, minimize the amount of time you spend talking to your team about the referees. There are plenty of other factors and variables to worry about during a game. Don't waste your time and energy worrying about what the officials are doing. And, save your lengthy post-game diatribes about the referees with the media as well. Be sure your philosophy on working with officials is imparted on your lower-level coaches as well. A ninth-grade basketball game is not the place for a freshman coach to berate a referee — everyone, including the referees — are there to learn.

Use this off-season time to think of

Coach/Referee Improvement Checklist

1. Minimize time spent with team discussing officials.
2. Minimize time discussing officials with the media.
3. Extend the aforementioned philosophies to all members of your coaching staff, including lower-level coaches.
4. Invite a referee to practice to discuss rules and the officiating process.
5. Invite a referee to a coaches' meeting to discuss rules and the officiating process.
6. Always include in your preseason work time to discuss rules changes with your players.
7. Always impart to your players that if they play as well as the officials officiate, you'll never lose.
8. Never berate an official during a game.
9. Remaining calm as a coach should guarantee that your players remain calm.
10. Instruct your captains that only one of them can address the officials during the action.

4

---

better ways to work with officials. Maybe invite a referee or two to an early season practice. Or, ask him or her to run a mini-clinic of rule changes and standard problem areas such as blocking vs. charging. Above all, teach your players that officials are people too.

6.4 April Is The Clinic Month

There are three areas of spring coaching clinics that the head coach needs to give his or her attention.

Sample Coaches' Clinic Format

FRIDAY, APRIL 21

4:00-5:00 p.m.	Registration and viewing of displays
5:30-6:30 p.m.	Bob Cimbollek — John Bapst H.S. (Maine) — Shooting: Is it a lost art? (demonstration)
6:45-7:45 p.m.	Bob Bigelow — Ex-Celtic — Overlooked basketball fundamentals
8:00-9:00 p.m.	George Blaney — Former coach, Seton Hall and Holy Cross — Man-to-man offenses
9:15-10:15 p.m.	Bob Brown — Bonny Eagle H.S. — Pressure defense: Half-court and full-court
10:30-11:30 p.m.	Jeff Meyer — Former coach, Liberty University — Special situations

SATURDAY, APRIL 22

8:30-9:00 a.m.	Coffee and doughnuts and viewing of displays
9:00-10:00 a.m.	George Blaney — Zone offenses
10:15-11:15 a.m.	Jeff Meyer — Beating the half-court trap
11:30-12:30 p.m.	Joanne Palombo-McCallie — Michigan State — Teaching the match-up zone
12:30-2:00 p.m.	Lunch; view displays
2:00-3:00 p.m.	Randy Dunton — Liberty University — Developing low-post play: Fundamentals and drills
3:15-4:15 p.m.	Len MacPhee — Rangeley H.S. (Maine) — Building a team defense
4:30-5:30 p.m.	Sandy Thomas — Athletes in Action — Teaching guard play
5:30-6:30 p.m.	Supper and viewing of displays
6:30-7:30 p.m.	Dennis Wolff — Boston University — The BU system offense
7:45-8:45 p.m.	Peter Webb — Maine Commissioner of Basketball — Understanding 3-person officiating (demonstration)
9:00-10:00 p.m.	Randy Dunton — Liberty's offensive and defensive system
10:15-11:15 p.m.	Bob Bigelow — Teaching big man and forward play (floor demonstration)

SUNDAY, APRIL 23

8:00-8:30 a.m.	Coffee and doughnuts and viewing of displays
8:30-9:30 a.m.	Dennis Wolff — The BU system defense
9:45-10:45 a.m.	Paul Vachon — Cony H.S. (Maine) – Teaching the run and jump press
11:00-12:00 p.m.	Dave Odom — South Carolina — Practice sessions
12:00-1:00 p.m.	Lunch and viewing of displays
1:00-2:00 p.m.	Dave Odom — South Carolina offensive system
2:15-3:15 p.m.	Sandy Thomas — Full-court press offense

5

Area No. 1 — Coaches should attend at least one instructional basketball clinic a year. April usually is the month for that. With accountability in coaching on the rise, most school districts strongly encourage their athletic coaches to attend a coaching clinic each year. Most state high school coaches associations offer annual instructional seminars or clinics. If you're coaching in a state that doesn't, find a clinic and take your staff. And, always try to come away from the clinic with one idea or concept to aid your program. Don't just make an appearance, then go off to socialize. Be professional. You just might learn something.

Area No. 2 — Coaches should speak at a coaching clinic at least once a year. There's no better teaching experience than preparing a lecture or demonstration for a group of your peers. Clinic talk keeps you fresh. Stick to a topic you know inside and out.

Area No. 3 — Coaches should run their own clinics from time to time. Putting together a coaching clinic is a great experience. Coaches should not try this task themselves. Select a group of your peers whom you can count on. Get sponsors for the event. Form 5 (previous page) lists typical topics for a coaching clinic. It is important to give variety to the proceedings and to remember that when coaches pay money or their districts pay money to send coaches, the even should be a professionally run operation.

6.5 Interviewing And Hiring Assistant Coaches

If you are a high school coach, perhaps your athletic director affords you the opportunity to be involved in the hiring process when you need to replace an assistant coach. Some do, some don't. The thoughtful administra-tor at the very least should allow the head coach to sit in the interview and provide input before the final selection is made.

Within the last 20 years or so, many high school basketball coaches come from outside the school system. Gone are the days when the varsity basket-ball coach taught physical education, the junior varsity coach taught history and the ninth grade coach was the jun-ior high health teacher.

If you get the opportunity to sit in on the interview, ask questions about the candidate's aspirations, philosophy, loyalty and knowledge of the game.

Question No. 1 — Aspirations? Find out the candidate's future plans in coaching. For example, you may be interviewing a young assistant, looking for experience before moving on to a varsity job. This is something you should know. And, even if the candidate comes to you with the reputation of being an outstanding player it does-n't mean he or she is going to make a great assistant. Sometimes they are, sometimes they aren't.

Question No. 2 — Philosophy? If you're a half-court offensive coach and the young person sitting in front of you thinks the fast break is the only way to play, you need to ask this person about his or her ability to adapt. Hiring a per-son who can't adapt can be disruptive to your team.

Question No. 3 — Loyalty? You want an assistant who is loyal to your system. You also want someone who is loyal to your team. For example, semi-retired former varsity coaches are typical

["You want an assistant who is loyal to your system. You also want someone who is loyal to your team."]

assistant-coaching candidates. Does this person still have varsity career plans? Can he or she play the role of assistant after years of running the show?

Question No. 4 — Knowledge? Another type of assistant-coach candidate is an older person who just wants to help. It is not out of the question to ask several basketball-related specifics such as diagramming press breakers or inbound plays. Word these questions in a manner so they are not personally offensive. When the season starts and duties are assigned, you'll be glad you took the time to plan the interview questions.

6.6 Rethinking Your Philosophy

One of the most difficult jobs in coaching is rethinking your philosophy of the game. A coach's personal philosophy regarding how the game should be played is a fairly nebulous variable. Most years, especially in small schools, the talent pool varies. You may consider yourself a defensive purist whose teams play single-coverage defense in the half-court at all times. Of course, a dilemma arises when a different defense is required. Consider these factors and decide if you need to reevaluate your coaching philosophy.

Factor No. 1 — Proper evaluation of personnel. This all goes back to the evaluation process. Day one of tryouts is when coaches see what they have. Analyzing what you view in the gym is not an easy task. The thoughtful coach is open to change. The best coaches meld their players around the system they perform best. Coaches who stubbornly brag they will fastbreak and press come hell or high water may find themselves in over their heads – no pun intended – a lot of seasons.

Factor No. 2 — Want to be a fast-break team? On the offensive end, if you want to run the floor, you must control the defensive boards. Size not always is the most significant variable in this type of philosophy but aggressive board play is. It is tough to run the floor without controlling the boards. Also, a fastbreak team needs to be proficient at perimeter scoring. Lots of opportunities require kick-outs and long-distance shooting. Finally, you'll need a true point guard who handles pressure, dribbles well, passes well and shoots well. Coaches who live and die by the break and don't have those three variables on their side are going to lose as many as they win. Rethinking your full-court philosophy may include instituting walk-the-ball scenarios for your team or even initiating a controlled break. The point is: Teaching your kids to recognize the difference between walking and running situations is a tough task.

Factor No. 3 — Staying in the half-court. Half-court teams need great floor generals. Lots of different players can assume a floor leadership role (refer to the leadership details in 6.1). Also, your team stands a better chance in the half-court if quickness and perimeter shooting aren't their best attributes.

Factor No. 4 — Rolling with the punches. Work with what you have and don't force players into situations where they can't win. Do you have quick guards and slower big men? Put them in a combination zone. You have to do whatever you can to get the most out of your players. For example, in 2003 Jim Boeheim of Syracuse rolled with the punches and stuck with the best defense for his team — a 2-3 zone

— and won the NCAA title.

Factor No. 5 – What about pressure? Small, quick teams apply a different variety of pressure than a bigger, slower one. But, either way, you should be able to take all types of players and have them press at times. If your team is big, start by teaching them a variety of zone presses so the big players move and attempt to intercept passes. Combine this philosophy with a half-court trap. Not all pressure comes in the full-court. Some teams apply the best pressure in the half-court. Half-court presses especially are effective when trying to take time off the clock (at the end of a half or game).

Factor No. 6 — Personnel management may be the key. Some defenses require coaches to use their bench. Not every player on your team performs every task well. There's nothing better in basketball than having two or three players who can spark your club by entering the game, getting into a press and leading the team to victory.

Factor No. 7 — Putting all this into perspective. Learning the right formula for success is not as easy as teaching one offensive and one defensive system each and every year. Roll with the punches. Change your plan when you need to and realize that you have kids on your bench who can help you in different situations.

Chapter 7

MAY: PREPARING FOR OFF-SEASON WORK

7.1 Interviewing Next Year's Participants

Bring in your next year's basketball participants and discuss areas of their basketball life, which you feel are important relative to next year's success. Most importantly, involve the high school coaching staff to make the process more effective. Never underestimate the significance of input in the overall scheme of things in your school. As head hoop boss, if you are of the mind that what you say or do is the be-all and end-all for your program, then you need a major attitude adjustment.

May is the perfect time for you and your staff to meet with the athletes who are in grades 9-11. You and your staff should have a good handle on each player's ability, and, perhaps most importantly, just what each kid needs to do to reach varsity status. The following are some key areas to discuss when having one-on-one meetings with players.

Area No. 1 — What they feel they need to improve. It's interesting to hear the kids discuss their hoop shortcomings. You'll be surprised how quickly they put the onus on themselves. Occasionally, you get a player who redirects the question at you.

Don't budge. The old psychological ploy of answering a question with a question shouldn't wash in your meeting. Ask kids to write out areas they need to improve. This gives you a written form to keep. An example is Form 1 on the next page.

Area No. 2 — Define weakness and give suggestions for improvement. Have a brief discussion about the player's weakness, then offer ways to improve that skill. A player may tell you that he or she wants to become a more serious threat as an outside shooter. Now, the player and the coach have to huddle and find a way to improve that skill. With summer ball on the horizon on the coaching calendar, both the coach and the player must find the time to work together to improve this important fundamental area of the game. Players will make time for improvement. To work with a player who wants to improve his or her shooting, follow Form 2 (page 81).

Area No. 3 — Offer written or film aids to enhance the process. I'm lucky, a number of years ago my wife Shelly had local carpenters build me a nice office where I could collect and store 33 years worth of hoop stuff. Coaches, players or whoever needs

Checklist for Self-Improvement

1. Please list what you consider your basketball strengths _____

_____

_____

_____

2. Please list what you consider your basketball weaknesses _____

_____

_____

_____

3. Position you currently play _____

_____

4. Position you aspire to play _____

_____

5. Amount of time devoted to basketball each day _____

_____

6. Amount of time devoted to individual skills improvement _____

_____

1

coaching material knows they can come to me. Try to do the same thing in your office by starting your own library. Keep as much supplemental material on hand as you can to aid in the teaching process. Make a trip to a local bookstore and buy a book to aid one of your player's desire to improve. Photocopy some of your own materials or loan out instructional videos. Form 3 (page 82) is a list of basketball coaching material (in alphabetical order) that should be in every coach's library.

Area No. 4 — Keep copies of what transpired in the meeting. Once you've defined the problem, documented it and produced material to aid instruction, then it is of equally vital importance that you put all of this in writing and produce a second copy for

"Keep as much supplemental material on hand to aid in the teaching process."

Shooting Needs Form

1. Footwork _____

_____

_____

2. Shooting form _____

_____

3. Areas of concern _____

_____

_____

4. Percentage player shot from the floor previous season _____

_____

5. Percentage player shot from the foul line previous season _____

_____

6. Best shot in player's repertoire _____

_____

7. Worst shot in player's repertoire _____

_____

8. Comments _____

_____

_____

2

the player. Whether you're a computer kind of coach (typed into a file with subsequent results) or an old-fashioned coach (catalogue all info, stuff it into a file and file it in a metal cabinet), it's important to keep track of these meetings. Record the date of the meeting, the subject of the meeting and all subsequent notes.

Area No. 5 — Avoid picking next year's team too soon. As you wrap up individual meetings with next year's basketball participants, it is critical not to pick next year's team too early. There are always kids who are pretty much a given but it is dangerous to

Bibliography Of Basketball Materials

1. Alford, Steve, **Basketball Guard Play,** 160 pages
2. Baumgartner, Dick, **Power and Timing Techniques for the Jump Shot and Free Throw,** 32 pages
3. Brown, Hubie, **Hubie on Basketball,** 152 pages
4. Cimbollek, Bob, **Basketball's Simplified & Scientific Methods Manual For Improving Perimeter Shooting Percentages,** 140 pages
5. Knight, Bob and Newell, Pete, **Basketball According to Knight and Newell,** Vol. 2, 186 pages
6. Krzyzewski, Mike, **Duke's Team Man-to-Man Defense,** 44 pages
7. Raveling, George, **War on the Boards**, 89 pages
8. Simpson, Sandy, **Coaching Girls' Basketball Successfully,** 272 pages
9. Smith, Dean, Basketball — **Multiple Offense and Defense**, 304 pages
10. Wooden, John, **Practical Modern Basketball,** 452 pages
11. Wooten, Morgan, **Coaching Basketball Successfully,** 225 pages

3

make promises you might not be able to keep. Never, unless you have a death wish for your job, make promises to future players about the amount of time they'll play in the upcoming season. Always tell your kids that the basketball season is an ongoing tryout. This keeps them on their toes.

7.2 Breaking Down Film

While some coaches like simply to view videotape, it's more of a service to you and your team to invest in the process. Many of your offensive and defensive problems are correctable with the proper use of videotape.

Every coach has a different philosophy for breaking down film. Some use it as a motivator for the players, telling them what they did correctly and they did incorrectly. Many times, that's fine. But, consider, you have an entire game at your disposal. You don't have to think back to certain situations because it's all right in front of you.

A good way to break down film starts with ascertaining how successful your motion offense was against a particular opponent's man-to-man. Do this with the help of your assistant(s).

Another area is to keep track of the possessions when you scored and missed. Figure out where on the floor you made shots and where you missed them (Form 4 next page).

Film breakdown is not complete until someone on staff keeps track of every play, every possession, make or miss...and this includes defense as well. Consider, you may love your half-court trap. A steal or two may have brought you and your assistants right out of your Florsheim tasseled loafers. But, after breaking down film, you may find that the opposition scored three times as often as you stole the ball or deflected a pass.

7.3 Evaluating Your Staff

You may hate meetings (I do) but the inherent responsibility of running a quality basketball program at the high school level requires meetings with the team and coaching staff. Staff evaluation is a must for a head coach and springtime is a good time to do this: The season still is fresh in everyone's mind. On a staff-evaluation level, refer back to your job descriptions (page 40) and dis-

Winning Hoops Academy Self-Evaluation Film Form

Opponent: _____   Date: _____

1. Number of possessions we scored: _____

_____

2. Offenses we scored the most: _____

_____

3. Offenses we scored the least: _____

_____

4. Defensive stops: _____

Form continues on next page

4

cuss what has or has not been done based on that initial assignment. Keep in mind specifics you discussed prior to the season with each of these coaches.

You might have a varsity assistant who does no more than cheer on the team — never underestimate the value of this coach. Other times, you might need a sounding board in the assistant's role (someone to bounce ideas off).

This coach can be equally important. This assistant coach who listens, especially after a loss, is a great asset.

Junior varsity and freshman coaches should be responsible for their own day-to-day coaching responsibilities, as well as a few other things (scouting) for the varsity. Just remember these people should not be bogged down with a college-type workload and never

Winning Hoops Academy Self-Evaluation Film Form - Cont'd

5. Best defense to stop opponent: _____

_____

6. press steals, turnovers, or poor shots: _____

_____

7. Best press stoppers: _____

_____

8. Comments: _____

_____

_____

9. Suggestions: _____

_____

_____

4

overlap your own responsibility.

For the actual evaluation process, individual sit-down sessions are most effective. Avoid telephone evaluations if possible. For example, if your junior varsity coach fails to follow a simple guideline such as playing all his players in every game — something you should have agreed upon in the fall — he needs to see and hear you discuss it. Another example of a coaching evalua-tion concern may have to do with the strength of the overall program versus individual career advancement. Having a face-to-face evaluation process cleans up a lot of these types of problems.

7.4 Self-Evaluation

For the high school coach especially, self-evaluation is a beneficial tool if for no other reason than being honest with yourself. After evaluating the rest of

> **"Self-evaluation is a beneficial tool if for no other reason than being honest with yourself."**

Self-Evaluation Form

Instructor _____ Program _____ Year _____

	LOW			HIGH	
1. HANDLING EQUIPMENT (management collection/issue)	1	2	3	4	5
2. RELATIONSHIP WITH PARENTS (appropriate rapport)	1	2	3	4	5
3. RELATIONSHIP WITH COMMUNITY (interested individuals)	1	2	3	4	5
4. PRE-GAME DETAILS (staff/team prepared for event)	1	2	3	4	5
5. STATISTICS (maintains adequate records)	1	2	3	4	5
6. ADHERENCE TO REGULATIONS (national, state, school)	1	2	3	4	5
7. RELATIONSHIP WITH MEDIA (balanced communication)	1	2	3	4	5
8. RELATIONSHIP WITH BUILDING STAFF (maintenance)	1	2	3	4	5
9. AWARENESS OF TRENDS (keeps informed of new concepts)	1	2	3	4	5
10. PRACTICE SUPERVISION (organizes, supervises, evaluates practices with attention to players mental and physical well-being)	1	2	3	4	5
11. RELATIONSHIP WITH ADMINISTRATION (loyalty)	1	2	3	4	5
12. DURING GAME BEHAVIOR (maintains self-control, sportsmanlike conduct with staff, players, officials)	1	2	3	4	5
13. AFTER GAME CONDUCT (accepts outcome of game in a professional manner)	1	2	3	4	5
14. RELATIONSHIP WITH PLAYERS (discipline is firm and fair, open communication, enforces rules and the athletic code)	1	2	3	4	5
15. INTEGRATION OF COACHING (fine community representative)	1	2	3	4	5
16. WILL GO THE EXTRA MILE (league meetings, hard work)	1	2	3	4	5

Commendations:

Suggestions for improvement:

Coach's Signature: _____

Athletic Director: _____

Date: _____

Coach's Comments:

5

Player Improvement Sheet
(Coach's Job Perspective)

Name	Position	Skill level 1-10 in fall	Skill level 1-10 in spring	Comments on job coach(es) did

6

the staff, it's a good idea to look at your own performance.

The obvious place to begin evaluating your own performance is with your won/loss record versus the talent available. This could be more difficult if you take the public's perception of how you "should have done" into play. For example, two seasons ago you had a 17-1 record and won the Eastern Maine title. But, later that year, you graduated nine seniors. So, last year, the younger kids only managed eight wins and lost in the preliminary round of the tournament. Was this a good season? Bad season? Your view of the season may be much different than the expectations of parents or of the administration. However, don't be swayed by outside opinion. You know your team. Go back to the individual tapes and be honest with yourself. Fill out a self-evaluation form honestly (Form 5, page 85).

Player improvement is critical area to your individual evaluation. Most of your time during the season is spent with game preparation but individual improvement always is a part of the package. Use Form 6 (previous page) as a player improvement form from your job perspective.

View tape on individual players if your memory fails you. Be honest with yourself again. Did you spend too much time on your half-court trap and not enough time on your center's free-throw technique? Only you are the judge of that.

Another valuable self-evaluation tool is getting another coach to look at your season. Inviting other coaches (of teams you don't play) to practice or games during the season to rate your performance helps. After the season, ask a respected coaching friend to view film. Demand honesty and return the favor if asked.

A final self-evaluation technique is to list your strengths and weaknesses. If man-to-man defensive instruction tops your list of strengths and half-court trap offenses top your list of weaknesses, spend more time honing up on trap offenses than on man techniques. Human nature dictates we spend more time working on what we're good at rather than the areas which need improvement.

7.5 Utilizing Your Off-Season Time

School's out. Vacation has started. Your heart says to give your basketball team the summer off. Your head tells you that you better not knowing full well that every opponent you play currently is putting in long hours getting ready for next season. Do you want to enroll your kids in an organized league? Didn't you play enough games during the season? Should they have some time off?

There are three concerns and considerations for basketball out-of-season training to consider.

Consideration No. 1 — Encourage your players to enroll in a summer camp. Don't be one of those coaches that only thinks his means of learning the finer points of the game is the only one that matters. Encourage your players to attend summer camps. If for no

[**"After the season, ask a respected coaching friend to view (your) film. Demand honesty..."**]

other reason than hearing someone else reinforce what you've been telling them for months, you should feel comfortable sending your players to another coach's camp. You should post camp brochures and encourage the work of others. You might be able to get your players a discount by volunteering your services as a counselor.

Never pressure your kids to attend camp. Many camps are expensive and you don't want to deal with that issue. Team fund-raisers might aid in the underwriting of camp expenses, especially if your individual interviews result in your team's desire to attend one of these so-called "team weeks."

Consideration No. 2 — What about these "team weeks"? A team week is when you and your team attend an abbreviated summer session together as one unit. These team weeks are gaining in popularity. They usually run 3-5 days in duration. Your team plays other teams, you have the opportunity to stick together while playing in a semi-pressure situation as a unit and to be together off the basketball floor as well. By planning a team week far enough in advance, it's easier for you, your assistants and your team members to raise money. A good time usually is had by all and a team week provides a sensible, viable option to making an entire summer commitment to a league (more on this in Chapter 7.6).

Consideration No. 3 – Encourage individual work. Provide your team members with an off-season workout sheet, which includes footwork, shooting drills, leg-strengthening exercises,

ball-handling drills and conditioning drills (Form 7 next page). Most high school players welcome the opportunity to have an organized, self-improvement program offered to them. Remember, don't push your kids. This is still vacation time. Stress family first to your players and you go a long way in enhancing the all-important variable of public relations that far too many coaches overlook. Rely on your individual sessions before school lets out to emphasize individual strengths and weaknesses.

7.6 Choosing A Team Weekend

If you decide to go the route of planning a team weekend, there are several variables to consider: price, what you get, referees and loose ends.

In regard to price, team weekends run in the neighborhood of $110-150 for each participant. Prices vary based on whether your team is staying overnight. Day rates always are cheaper. Inquire about meal cost relative to the overall expense of the camper and be aware that a night or two in the dorm is going to set you and your kids back a few dollars. Beware of pricey events, it's difficult enough to strap your players with an overall participation fee for the summer. By adding weekend-type affairs, players get bogged down.

After considering price, figure out what you and your team are receiving with that price. You should look for a team weekend that gives your players at least five or six games. If you're looking for a camp that develops team

[**"Remember, don't push your kids. This is still vacation time."**]

Summer Workout Sheet

Activity	Date	Reps	Comments on your work
Foul shots			
Free shooting			
Leg Strengthening exercises (see Sept.)			
Actual playing			
Dribbling			
Passing			
Running			

7

continuity and unity, then you want a place that gives you some bang for the buck. Hesitate to enter camps only guaranteeing a couple of games.

Once you determine the cost and number of games, next ask who will be refereeing the games. Be cautious about taking your team to a team weekend where college kids are blowing the whistle. After all, the high cost of camp combined with the heated atmosphere of a high school game necessitates certified officials. You want your team to come away from the event with improved skills and not a penchant for rough games, which is what usually breaks out when college kids are officiating.

Tying up loose ends also is a key to a successful team weekend. Make sure the advertising lives up to its claim. If a free swim is advertised, make sure it's supervised and that you and your team get one each day. And, be cautious about meals. Don't let your players live on food dispenser junk food. If three meals a day are advertised, then that's what you should get. Most of all, enjoy the time together, get something out of it and have fun.

Help Your Players Learn The Fundamentals!

Rebounding *(24 pages)* $11.95
Every coach knows that rebounding is often the critical difference between having a very competitive team and one that's a perennial loser. This 24-page report features articles and drills from 23 outstanding coaches around the world. You'll find articles on offensive and defensive rebounding, rebounding tips, box-out techniques, coaching techniques, drills, securing missed free throws and preparing players for the mental aspect of battling for loose balls.

The Secrets Of Passing *(16 pages)* $9.95
Teach your players the art of passing the basketball with this outstanding coaching report. Written by some of today's top coaches, this report is filled with articles, drills and teaching techniques to improve your team's ball movement and to cut down on those aggravating turnovers. Articles include ways of teaching your players how to feed the ball into the post, developing good pass-catching hands, advanced passing concepts, improving your team's transition passing and 27 fantastic individual and team passing drills. Uncover all the hidden secrets of passing with this valuable report!

Stoppers!
Time-Tested Defensive Drills *(16 pages)* $9.95
Looking for rock-solid defensive drills that will turn your players into ball-hawking defensive stoppers? You'll get a proven 7-on-5 drill that prepares your players for live-game action, shell drills, a 3-on-3 drill sequence that teaches half-court man-to-man defense, drill games that spice up any practice, charge drills, helpside drills, defensive intensity and hustle drills, defensive transition drills, fundamental drills and much more! A comprehensive report for coaches who are looking for drills that will immediately improve their defenses.

Fundamental Dribbling *(8 pages)*....................$7.95
Read an exciting 8-page Special Coaching Report that contains right-to-the-point, highly valuable information from an outstanding high school coach that will definitely help your players improve their dribbling techniques. This in-depth ballhandling report details specific dribbling tips specifically aimed at individual players at every position, 13 moves to get away from defensive pressure, dribbling drills and more!

Priority Code: WHCDCG

LESSITER PUBLICATIONS SHIPPING CHART

ORDER AMOUNT	ECONOMY 5-8 day delivery (shipped USPS)	CANADA
Up to $20	$ 3.95	$ 5.95
$21 to $50	$ 5.95	$ 7.95
$51-100	$ 6.95	$ 8.95
$101-$150	$ 8.95	$11.95
$151-$200	$ 9.95	$13.95
$201 and Up	$11.95	$15.95

International: Minimum charge $15.75. Orders $51-$300: 25% of total order plus $3 handling charge
Orders over $300: 18% of total plus $3 handling charge. Actual postage charge if amount exceeds 25% or 18% amount.

MAIL TO: *Winning Hoops,* P.O. Box 624, Brookfield, WI 53008-0624
FOR FASTER SERVICE: Call: (866) 839-8455 (U.S. and Canada only) or (262) 432-0388
Fax: (262) 786-5564 • E-mail: info@lesspub.com • **Web site:** www.winninghoops.com

Chapter 8

JUNE: SUMMER PLAY BEGINS

8.1 High School Summer Ball: Play Your Kids

Let's be clear on summer ball — do not treat these games like they are the finals of the state basketball tournament and leave kids on the end of the bench without having a chance to play.

Most summer basketball participants play in the off-season to improve their skills and to have fun. The enjoyment level diminishes quickly if coaches treat the game process solely as a vehicle to win. You owe every kid who has laid down cash, gone through the process of getting a physical — and perhaps more importantly taken time off from work — the opportunity to participate in games.

The process of playing your kids is not a difficult one to master. For the sake of argument, say you have 15 kids on your squad. Regardless of your opponent you should either platoon your team or substitute early enough to give your players a fair shake on the floor (see Form 1 next page).

Don't run four or five kids into the ballgame with less than a minute left if they haven't played all game. If you do this, don't expect them to come back. In today's world, kids have so much

going on in their lives (more than we did) that any insult to a participant might be enough to turn them off from the game entirely. After all they put a lot into being on the team, who could blame them?

I have an old friend who is a well-known college coach in Maine (Jim Graffam) who plays all of his kids in every regular season and postseason game. He says that players practice harder, take their roles more seriously and have more fun when they know they're going to play every game. This is something to keep in mind as you progress through the summer. Team camaraderie and unity are key variables in June and July, as well as December and January.

8.2 Making Time For Individual Instruction

The bane of high school hoop coaches is the amount of time invested in our program with team-orientated instruction. Stick your head in any gym in the region during the winter months and you're likely to find a lecture from a coach resulting in a team concept. Half-court trap offenses, press breakers and half-court plays top a long list of areas head coaches cover nightly with

Summer Basketball Platoon Chart

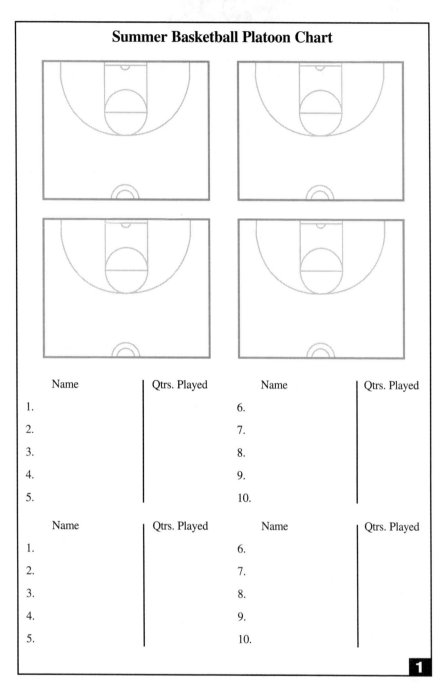

Name	Qtrs. Played	Name	Qtrs. Played
1.		6.	
2.		7.	
3.		8.	
4.		9.	
5.		10.	

Name	Qtrs. Played	Name	Qtrs. Played
1.		6.	
2.		7.	
3.		8.	
4.		9.	
5.		10.	

1

their players for the all-important regular season games.

The problem is that individual instruction suffers and, for the most part, skill teaching takes a backseat to team-orientated work. Time always is vital in coaching. A 90-minute or two-hour time slot often is not enough to work on individual skills, especially if the coach wants one-on-one time with the player. The following are key skills to highlight and the methods to get the job done.

Skill No. 1 — Identifying weakness. Meet with the kids and identify areas of their game that need work. This goes back to having players fill out goal cards (Chapter 1.8). Most players are anxious to improve. Even those who are highly skilled want to be better and it is incumbent upon the coach to set up a plan to get the job done.

Skill No. 2 — Finding time. In the off-season during your summer program, take time to work with individuals early in the practice or before the game, then employ what you've just taught in drill form with the entire team. That spreads the value of the lesson and it helps minimize the embarrassment of being singled out. Use June to find time to work on individual skills so you won't have to worry about it in November.

Skill No. 3 — Listing often-overlooked individual skills. Shooting technique, or lack of it, tops a length list of individual skills work that is ignored far too often. Here's a rule of thumb when it comes to shooting instruction: Do not touch a senior's shooting technique. Unless a player has an elbow sticking out on his free-throw technique, chances are an 18-year-old is less likely to be receptive to change. All other players are fair game. With younger kids, shooting technique from the floor up needs scrutiny. It's surprising to see how much a shot improves when a player becomes properly aligned to the target.

Ball-handling runs a close second to shooting woes. Not every player in your program is a point guard but all players, at one time or another, are going to be called upon to dribble under pressure. So, all players need some level of competence in this skill area. Full-court drills with dribbling never hurt anyone's dexterity level and by encouraging your kids to handle a ball every chance they get, you're well on your way to improving this skill. In his early days at the University of Maryland, Lefty Driesell required all of his players to have a basketball with them at all times so they could have a good feel for the ball. This might be extreme but it could help your players develop better ball-handling skills on their own time.

Skill No. 4 — Documenting skills. Coaches need to keep track of players' individual skill needs and improvement in summer. Use Form 3 on the next page as a guide.

8.3 So You've Been Asked To Speak At A Summer Camp...

Take advantage of being asked to speak to young people at summer camps, banquets and clinics. It is high praise to have a captive audience to impart the modicum of hoop wisdom you've picked up through the years. Camps are a great experience for staff, guest lecturers and campers. But, speak-

[**"Do not touch a senior's shooting technique...an 18-year-old is less likely to be receptive to change."**]

Summer Skills Rating Sheet

Rate 1-10: 1 being poor; 10 being outstanding

Name	Ball-handling	Perimeter Shooting	Inside Shooting	Foul Shooting	Defense	Rebounding	Attitude	Passing

3

ers need to know a few important variables prior to entering the speaker's role.

Variable No. 1 — Put some thought into the preparation of the speech. Kids may be the toughest audience on the planet and a shoddy effort on your part is sure to have players snoozing quickly. There's nothing worse than boring your audience. Also, concentrate on time management. Treat your presentation like a practice and it is sure to flow smoothly. Don't try to wing it – be prepared.

Variable No. 2 — Keep lecture time to a minimum. Keeping in mind that young people come to camps to play basketball, speakers must be aware that lengthy presentations fall on deaf ears in 10 minutes or so. A hot gym…sitting on a cold floor…listening to a guest speaker recount his or her life story to a group of campers (who may have just come from a full-court game or station work)…it's a recipe for disaster.

Variable No. 3 — Get the campers up and moving. Following a brief lecture, incorporate action within the pres-

45-Minute Camp Presentation

1. 10 minutes	Thank those who invited you and give background on yourself and subject at hand.
2. 5 minutes	Pick someone out of the crowd and demonstrate with you the skill topic of the day.
3. 10 minutes	Station work, supervised by you at all six stations and by camp counselors at each station.
4. 5 minutes	Return to group setting; either add to or correct what you just witnessed on the floor.
5. 10 minutes	Group drill.
6. 5 minutes	Contests.
7. Closing remarks.	

4

entation of drills or group work to get players involved. Players are restless after the initial speech, so involve them early and assign duties. They're there to work and your camp time should not be rest time for them. The same holds true for the camp director and/or staff. Speakers often need help with demonstrations and if the camp crowd is large, then staff members are important.

Variable No. 4 — Individual demonstration to highlight skills. Following the lecture and the group involvement, a successful technique to enhance your previous work is to target campers who demonstrate some expertise in the area of concern and also campers who don't. With the group sitting around one basket, use the skilled players to demonstrate how to perform the skill. Be sure to bring in the less skilled players to run through the technique as well. This shows to those in attendance that this skill is not as easy

as it seems. Be positive with the less skilled players and encourage them as they work on the technique.

Variable No. 5 – Always end on a positive note. Bring a few door prizes to your lectures to enhance and reward performance. Wrist bands, NERF balls, T-shirts and any printed materials on the skills in question are great items to carry to your camp work. It doesn't take much to please a kid and your kind approach to wrapping up a session goes a long way in helping the camp's reputation. The above form (Form 4) shows a typical camp session schedule to follow.

8.4 Overuse Of Stations At Summer Camp

Much like reducing the time spent at practice when entering the month of January, if you're running a summer camp, don't go overboard and schedule all of the players' time for station work. Station work is important and players know they will be taking part in some of these exercises at camp. But, limiting the use of stations keeps things crisper and keeps player more interested in what you're teaching. Plus, remember one of the reasons why these players chose your camp – fun. Here are some do's and don'ts for station work at a camp.

Do's

1. Keep lectures brief.
2. Keep kids moving.
3. Make sure everyone tries the "new" skill.
4. Avoid letting highly skilled kids dominate the proceedings.
5. Take water breaks together.

Don'ts

1. Don't talk too much.
2. Don't allow kids to sit while others work.
3. Don't forget about kids who are reluctant to participate. Take them to a side basket for one-on-one attention.
4. Don't make a hero out of someone. Always give out equal praise.
5. Don't allow sports drink consumption during station work.

These do's and don'ts may sound easy but keep them in mind at all times. The best stations are staffed by caring workers who understand that not every camper is ready for professional basketball. The theme of summer work is fun. Fun is not talking down to campers who aren't as highly skilled. Fun is making contests out of skill areas and do it by teams. Fun is having the person in charge of the station to participate in the drill. Kids enjoy seeing an adult's ability but they get kick out of watching an adult struggle a bit.

8.5 Kids Have Families Too

Players need to be given appropriate, ample time to spend with their loved ones during vacation months. Far too many summer basketball programs run from the day after school gets out until the Sunday before fall sports begin. Look for a summer program that offers about six weeks of play including playoffs for about 12-14 games.

In states like Maine, where I have spent most of my life, good weather is not always the norm in the off-season months. Families and their scheduled vacation activities always should be given top priority by the coach. Plus, many high school students work in the summertime. Over-scheduling them is going to make the "vacation" months more of a stressor than they need to be. Players only get to be young once, so let them take advantage of it.

Chapter 9

JULY: WINDING DOWN OFF-SEASON WORK

Summer programs are in the wrap-up stage by the end of July. Players need anywhere between 2-4 weeks to get ready for the rigors of fall sports. Even players who don't participate in fall sports (you should encourage all athletes to play sports other than basketball) need some downtime too.

9.1 Making Sense Of Summer Work

Evaluate your off-season programs and organize them as if they were regular-season affairs. Focus on the following areas to take advantage of the time your players put into basketball during the off-season.

Focus No. 1 — List strengths and weaknesses. Evaluating players before and after a summer program helps you ascertain if a player has mastered a skill or not. Sure, summertime is less hectic than the winter schedule but a written record of a particular player's strengths and weaknesses aids you come fall. Kids who have not participated in a summer program should be listed too with special emphasis on that player's strengths and weaknesses. The form on the next page (Form 1) is a good guide for evaluating players.

Focus No. 2 — Written evaluations. While you are keeping track of players' strengths and weaknesses, also put an overall summary of their summer work in writing. In the evaluation, thank the player for all of his or her hard work and applaud strengths while diplomatically pointing out areas that still need to be addressed. Also, take this opportunity to provide all players with a few helpful hints or drills so they can work on skills on their own time (Form 2, next page).

Focus No. 3 — Address team needs. Individual players need evaluation but the team as a whole needs evaluation as well (Form 3, page 100). Failure to evaluate the team diminishes the significance of playing organized games in the summer. Summer games are more laid back but they still deserve your time. Give these games the proper attention by writing a perspective of your perceptions of the team's progress.

[**"Players need anywhere between 2-4 weeks to get ready for the rigors of fall sports."**]

```
┌─────────────────────────────────────────────────────────┐
│               Post-Summer Evaluation Form                │
│ Name: _____                    │
│                                                           │
│ 1. Record of attendance: _____ │
│    _____ │
│                                                           │
│ 2. Attitude:_____ │
│    _____ │
│                                                           │
│ 3. Desire to learn: _____ │
│    _____ │
│                                                           │
│ 4. Potential contribution for fall: _____ │
│    _____ │
│                                                           │
│ 5. Strengths: _____ │
│    _____ │
│                                                           │
│ 6. Weaknesses: _____ │
│    _____ │
│                                                           │
│ 7. Comments: _____ │
│    _____ │
│    _____ │
│    _____ │
│                                                      [1]  │
└─────────────────────────────────────────────────────────┘
```

Focus No. 4 — Address staff needs. Your staff needs to be evaluated as well. Set clear parameters for lower-level coaches. Did you find one of your assistant coaches was less than enthusiastic about helping you? Keep track of that conduct (Form 4, page 101). Documenting every aspect of your program keeps you ahead of the game and provides you with a helpful tool for evaluation.

Focus No. 5 – Correspondence. A good way to put a wrap on your summer work is to correspond with players, coaches, referees, league directors, camp people, parents and others who have helped you along the way. It means a lot to people to receive a note from a coach. If you are going to put in the hours in the off-season, then you need to lend some of your regular-season professionalism to this time. Forms 5-10 on the next several pages provide examples of correspondence to different people within your basketball life.

9.2 To Thine Own Self Be True

July is a great time for reflection. Take some time to think about where you've been, where you are and where you're going. We've all had our own experiences and, if you don't mind, I'd like to give you my reflections on a

Post-Summer Summary Form (Player)

Name: _____

1. Summary of summer work: _____

_____

_____

_____

_____

_____

2. Potential spot for fall: _____

_____

_____

3. Other comments: _____

_____

_____

_____

_____

2

coaching career covering 33 years.

I've seen a myriad of changes in coaching in my career, one which began in 1969, and finished up in 2004. As I look at that span, I realize that I've been doing this for some time. I survived the hairstyles of the '60s and '70s. And, I survived the overall looseness in society, which accompanied that dreadful, post-hippy look.

Ever-vigilant, I required my players to dress and act like they were playing in the 1950s. Granted, I rolled with the dress-code punches, and, of course, the sideburns — gosh, even I had some awful-looking ones. My wife keeps a 1973 photo of me as coach for when I get on one of my soapbox/lecture moods about how all my players were clean-shaven, hair-neat, etc.

Changes in this coaching business since my first high school varsity job also include the increased role parents now have in the proceedings of high school ball. Gone are the days when coach was king. Gone, too, are the days when teachers and coaches made decisions that were never questioned. In today's world, basketball season is an open season on coaches. From bickering at the supper table to outright confrontations with parents after games, the landscape of the whole profession has changed. And that is sad.

"In today's world, basketball season is an open season on coaches."

Summer Team Performance Sheet

Team: _____

Date: _____

Summer Record: _____

1. Summary: _____

_____

_____

_____

_____

_____

2. Surprises: _____

_____

_____

_____

3. Disappointments: _____

_____

_____

_____

3

I'm old enough to remember a time when what the coach said and did was law. End of discussion. Today, even administrators — the lousy ones at least — listen to parents to first and if they have time they hear the coach's side of the story. I lump these weak-kneed ADs and principals into one group: I call them the people whose next opinion is based on their last phone call.

Fortunately for me my last stint on the journey of coaching kids was with two people who were top-notch, sup-portive administrators. They provided a good base for a final fling in basketball. I've heard stories from colleagues who were not as lucky as I was. In fact, reflecting back on my career, most of the principals and ADs I've had were very supportive. For that, I can be thankful.

Another key factor representing change in coaching since I began has been the increase of club teams that now are dotting the map in Maine (and I'm sure everywhere else). AAU stands atop any list I could make about prob-

["AAU stands atop any list I could make about problem areas for the high school coach."]

Summer Team Performance Sheet (Coaches)

Name: _____

Position held at school: _____

1. Coaching strengths: _____

_____

_____

_____

2. Coaching weaknesses: _____

_____

_____

_____

3. Summary: _____

_____

_____

_____

4. Suggestions for improvement: _____

_____

_____

_____

4

lems areas for the high school coach. Far too many youngsters are getting an overblown opinion of their own self-worth and ability, hoop-wise, in this grand game of ours. Then, they reenter the high school gym, thinking they are better than they actually are.

The ratings these club teams put on players are not accurate. They are done to increase attendance and membership in that particular club's organization. I had a player a couple of years ago rated No. 11 in the state but who didn't get as much as an honor beyond becoming a conference all-star for our team. Now, make no mistake about it, this kid was a solid high school participant but far too many of his peers are entering the college scene overrated and, quite frankly, not ready for the level of play to which they aspire.

For coaches, my final thought is this: You need to be true to yourself and to your beliefs from the time you enter this profession until the time you leave it. An old AD friend of mine

["You need to be true to yourself and to your beliefs..."]

Referee Correspondence

Dear Official:

On behalf of our players and coaches, I want to take this opportunity today to thank you for the many hours you have given this summer to help make our games quality affairs.

I have been involved in enough summer programs in my career to know that without good officiating, the games have a tendency to be rough and can get out of control quickly.

To you veteran officials, please know that the hours you have given us go a long way in not only helping our players get better but also help them avoid the development of bad habits.

To you younger officials, any opportunity you have as you mature in the business to be in a varsity setting, regardless of the time of year, goes a long way in helping you improve as an official.

Sincerely,

Ron Brown
Varsity Basketball Coach
Winning Hoops Academy

5

taught me well when he said always to remember that you as a coach have more to offer than they as a school district have to offer you. I've dug my heels in the same more than once and walked away from situations that were not good. Never let a school district tell you how to play or who to play. Expect backing in all disciplinary situations. Expect your administrators to keep parents at bay.

And finally, take pride in being part of this profession. Treat it like the priesthood or the ministry. There are a

League Director Correspondence

Dear League Director:

I can't tell you what a great time my players, coaches and I had participating in your summer basketball league. Everyone involved in your program was professional and polite.

We especially are grateful that you hired certified, board officials to referee our games. The kids were thrilled at the quality of prizes you provided to contest winners and league champions.

You can count on my telling every basketball person I meet that your summer league was the best one I have seen in a long, long time.

Please be sure to add our school to your mailing list for other camp events you may host.

Sincerely,

Ron Brown
Varsity Boys Basketball Coach
Winning Hoops Academy

6

Summer Wrap-Up Parent Letter

Dear Parents:

I wanted to take a minute today to thank each of you for your cooperation in accommodating the dates of our summer basketball program.

I caution each of our players that you are not a glorified taxi service. We have tried diligently to keep you and your family abreast of not only what we are doing and when we're doing it, but also of any changes in our schedule.

The future is bright indeed for our basketball program at Winning Hoops Academy, and in large part, you are responsible for all of that.

I have enjoyed my time with your kids and I am especially looking forward to the new season this fall.

Sincerely,

Ron Brown
Varsity Boys Basketball Coach
Winning Hoops Academy

7

lot of eyes and ears following your every move and your every word. What kind of example are you providing your own players? If you frequent bars — and I frown on that practice — then frequent them out of town. Keep your personal life, personal. Whether you like it or not, you are the center of attention in town, especially during the winter months. Set an example of

Summer Wrap-Up Player Letter

Dear Players:

Please excuse the formality of this correspondence but I wanted to contact each of you today and than you for the many hours you have put into basketball this summer.

As we have discussed many times in practice, commitment to improvement is an important variable in any success we have.

By now each of you should have your workout sheets. Please itemize and keep track of all activities you do.

There are great things on the horizon for the Winning Hoops Academy basketball program. You are an important part of that program and the effort you made this summer goes a long way in not only your own improvement, but also the improvement of our team.

Keep me posted on any needs you may have the rest of the summer.

I'm looking forward to seeing all of you in school.

Sincerely,

Ron Brown
Varsity Boys Basketball Coach
Winning Hoops Academy

8

Summer Wrap-Up Coaches Letter

Dear Coaches:

Thank you for your extra effort and time you gave our basketball program this summer.

By now, you know that I am a stickler for detail and having each of our assistants with us this summer is an important part of the process.

I also hope that each of you learned something this summer. As you know, I try to delegate responsibilities to all coaches, even in the vacation months.

Basketball has become a year-long activity. It is important that every coach in our program understands that notion and it is especially important that we act as a team to prepare diligently for what lies ahead.

I tell you truthfully when I say to you our program wouldn't be what it is today without you.

Sincerely,

Ron Brown
Varsity Boys Basketball Coach
Winning Hoops Academy

9

excellence in all you do. Quite frankly, even the most winning coach must do so because a lot of great ones have before you and you can soil the profession for others by being a bonehead just one night.

Yes, summer is a good time for thought. Reflection never killed anyone, did it?

9.3 Practice Organization: Are You Doing It?

Although regarded as a mundane topic in a lot of circles, practice organization for the high school basketball coach is of vital importance to the program's success. There's no better time than July to think this over. The day-to-day grind of coaching this sport takes tedium to a new level without proper planning. Use July as a time of reflec-

tion on philosophy and implementation.

Organization Topic No. 1 — Lesson plans are not silly. Never insult or short-change those who have hired you by being anything but efficient in practice planning. If you are a teacher, then you know how important a lesson plan is for the classroom. Carry this over to you daily instruction in the gymnasium.

Organization Topic No. 2 — Solid lesson plans include timed portions. When figuring out how properly to administer a 90-minute or two-hour practice in the winter, you need to allow specific lots of time for certain areas of instruction (Form 11, page 106).

Try being more efficient by cutting your station work time down to 5- to 10-minute segments. Remember, kids get bored easily. The coach who con-

["Never insult or short-change those who have hired you by being anything but efficient in practice planning."]

Correspondence With All Summer Staff

Dear Camp Workers:

I wanted to drop each of you a note today to thank you for the many hours you have put in with our basketball program.

Having had a few summer jobs myself, I know that a lot of days, we'd all enjoy being at the beach more than being the gym.

It's always gratifying to me to walk into our facility to see the floors swept, the equipment out and ready for use, and watching you – the staff – ready and eager to go for another session.

I am very fortunate to be surrounded by so many fine young people.

I look forward to seeing all of you again in school and please know that if there is anything I can do to help you along the way, don't hesitate to give me a call.

Go Wildcats!

Sincerely,

Ron Brown
Varsity Boys Basketball Coach
Winning Hoops Academy

10

centrates on time management goes a long way in determining how to get everything he or she wants to teach in that particular practice session.

Organization Topic No. 3 — Add a skill each night. Admit it, you've spent too much time drilling and scrimmaging in your practices. The easiest thing to do is to roll out the basketball and just let them play. Kids want to race up and down the floor every chance they get. It's more fun than listening to you and that day's teaching unit. But, if you're just continuing to keep your kids in shape, you're wasting valuable practice time. Try to add one thing daily in the preseason — either individual or team — and once the regular season begins, try to clean up one weakness or add a team skill that either needs brushing up or correcting entirely.

Organization Topic No. 4 — Foul shooting. Shoot two sets of 25 foul shots every night. Those 25 shots should be consecutive and have peers on the lane to simulate in-game free-throw attempts. Reach the point in your coaching where the majority of what you do imitates situations your kids face in real games.

Organization Topic No. 5 — Save film work and lectures for the classroom. Don't waste precious practice time watching film and lecturing about such sundry items as discipline and decorum. If you're scheduled for a 90-minute practice session the night before the big game, schedule a wrap-up session for talking about everything in your classroom or the cafeteria. You even can go as far as running your offense in the corridor or cafeteria with a pillow-type basketball to not take away valuable time from gym use.

Organization Topic No. 6 — Keep a journal. Keeping a journal (Form 12, page 107) is useful as you work your

Sample Practice Lesson Plan

1. Brief overview of plan for the day.
2. Outline verbally and on the floor the demonstration plan for the day.
3. Implement plan out on the floor.
4. Always include all players during the instructional stage of the unit.
5. Avoid having your best players — skills-wise — always together, especially in the teaching phase of the instructional unit.
6. Scrimmage briefly in the half-court, concentrating on the unit for today.
7. If you're comfortable with what you see in the half-court, extend the unit into full-court time.
8. Continue practice with drills, etc.
9. Wrap-up practice by reviewing the teaching unit for today.
10. Ask players to put the specific skill, play, offense or defense into their playbooks and enhance that teaching with a handout to supplement the unit they have just learned.

11

way through the summer. Jot down a few ideas so you don't forget about them later in the year.

9.4 How To Win On The Road

Another summer activity includes assessing problem areas such as how to win on the road. Sure, you love playing games in your home gym. You and your players establish a routine and there's nothing like eating your own food, sleeping in your own bed and playing in your own gym. Road trips are another matter. You should

approach away games differently from home games and overnight road trips should be approached in a different manner. Approaching road games can be tedious work. There are several key components to ponder to be successful away from the friendly confines of your home gymnasium.

Road Component No. 1 — Know the surroundings. Playing on the road never should be a shot in the dark. You should check out the facility and the surrounding components that will factor into the game. Look at the baskets to ascertain which one has the least amount of orange paint. The less orange paint, the more the home team has practiced on this particular hoop. Surprise the opposition by choosing that end of your second-half action. The rim will be looser and you'll get more bounces. Other things to consider are if the locker rooms are too hot or the baselines are too close to the walls.

Road Component No. 2 — Know the philosophy of the officiating board in that area. Refereeing changes when you hit the road. Rule interpretations in areas such as contact varies from officiating board to board. Different places have produced refs who call the games in their own, unique way.

Road Component No. 3 — Strike a routine despite the trip. Create a routine for players to offset the hurried nature of road trips (Form 13, next page). Give them a road-trip schedule. Meet with the team prior to boarding the bus. This is when you should share your itinerary for the trip. Provide par-

[**"The less orange paint, the more the home team has practiced on this particular hoop."**]

Coaches Daily Diary of Basketball Activities

1. Today's date: _____

_____

2. Activity summary: _____

_____

_____

3. Problems: _____

_____

_____

4. Comments: _____

_____

_____

5. Suggestions for improvement: _____

_____

_____

12

Road Game Checklist For Players

Opponent: _____ Destination: _____

Date: _____ Departure time: _____

1. Do I have all my equipment?
2. Did I pack a snack?
3. Did I bring money for stopover following the game?
4. Did I remind my parents that we take the bus to the game and come home on the busy from the game as a group?
5. Make sure we sit together as a group on the bus.
6. Make sure we sit together as a group in the opponent's gym.
7. Make sure we minimize noise to the game and from the game.
8. When we're in the building, we travel in groups of three or four to the restroom.
9. No self-guided tours of the grounds allowed.
10. We were dressed up when we got here and we'll look the same way when we leave.

13

Player Scouting Form

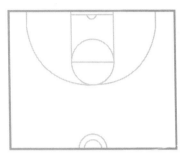 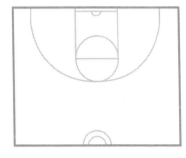

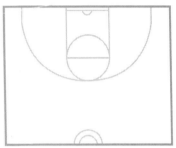 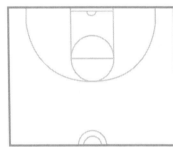

Score by period: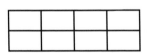

1. What would you do if you were coaching our team to play this opponent?

_____

_____

2. Opposing player(s) who you feel need special attention: _____

_____

3. What are the opponent's primary defenses? _____

_____

_____

4. Areas of concern: _____

_____

5. Comments: _____

_____

14

ents copies of the itinerary as well –
they'll appreciate it. Departure and
arrival times top your list.

**Road Component No. 4 — Take
your players scouting with you.** From
time to time, take players with you to
see the opposition. Keep this practice
in moderation as players have homework and other responsibilities. Going
to scout shows your players what you
do and they also get to see some of the
things you've discussed (Form 14, previous page). Many times, your players
come up with suggestions for game
preparation that surprise you.

**Road Component No. 5 — Trip
preparation.** The travel portion of
playing a game on the road needs to be
addressed. Scouting and hard work go
down the tubes if your team is not
ready for the trip itself. With high
school players, a few road rules are
vital to success:

1. Always have your team sit together on the bus.

2. Music only is allowed on individual music players with headsets.

3. Talking is kept to a minimum,
especially on the way to the game.

4. Getting in a game frame of mind
is difficult with too much frivolity.

5. The team sits together on the bus
until you give them a pre-game before
entering the gym.

**Road Component No. 6 —
Building conduct.** Nothing fouls up a
week of preparation for the big road
game like antics during the preliminary
contest. Have your team sit together
again during the junior varsity game or
whatever contest precedes yours.

Road Trip Do's & Don'ts For Players

1. Arrive 15 minutes before scheduled
departure time.

2. Don't be late or we'll leave without
you.

3. If you miss the bus, you might as
well go home.

4. No player can be transported to an
away game by his or her vehicle or a
parent's vehicle – EVER!

5. We are guests not only on the busy
but in the opponent's gym – act
accordingly.

6. Clean the bus before we get off it to
play.

7. Get a trash bag from the bus driver
and recheck the job you did cleaning.
No exceptions.

8. No music unless you have a headset.

9. Only eat snacks in the gym if the
school's rules permit.

10. Keep socializing with members of
the opposing crowd to a minimum.

15

Whether they're wearing warm-ups or
dress clothes, by wearing the same
things and sitting together, they put off
a posture of success. The opposition
sees that, the fans see that and the other
coaches see that, which shows your
team means business (see Form 15
above).

**Road Component No. 7 — When
to dress.** Every player has his or her
own routine for getting dressed before
the game. The problem is when players
get to the locker room too quickly and

**["Scouting and hard work go down the tubes if your
team is not ready for the trip itself."]**

spend too much time in there before the game. Anxiety builds and even the calmest player can come unglued. Unless they all need to be taped by the trainer, players should not go in to dress until halfway through the third period of the game prior.

Road Component No. 8 — Taking the floor. On the road, be the first one to come out of the chute. Most home teams prefer to take the floor last anyway and by coming out early you get acclimated to the surroundings.

Road Component No. 9 — The game itself. Keeping the crowd out of the game is of paramount importance. Keeping an even keep emotionally is a good way to enhance this process. Crowds react to a variety of things besides their teams' baskets. If your players complain to officials (which they shouldn't do anyway), taunt the opposition or respond to crowd noise – your team is in for a long night. Try to get your players to react the same way no matter what – win or lose, good call or bad call, or basket or miss.

Road Component No. 10 — After the game. Win or lose, sportsmanship is a must. The lasting impression you and your team makes on the road often is the only impression people have of your program. From the gym to the restaurant afterward, have your team be polite. You'd be surprised how quickly an isolated remark or incident is blown out of proportion.

Chapter 10

AUGUST: SCHOOL STARTS

10.1 Back To Class Checklist

With the start of school on the horizon, it's time to tidy up the recently completed summer program and start thinking like a high school coach again. Coach another sport if the opportunity presents itself. Don't spread yourself so thin that energy is depleted to the point that the basketball coaching process suffers.

August is a good time of year to make a list of things to be done to prepare for the upcoming basketball season. Examples of these things include schedules, grades for players and athletic equipment.

Use August as a time to huddle up with your athletic director and double-check your upcoming varsity schedule. By this time, most school athletic schedules are complete but there always is an exception. Don't walk into a problem by failing to check your schedule for snafus.

When it comes to the grades of your players, leave nothing to guesswork. Don't take a teenager's assessment of his or her academic standing at face value. Most kids do a bang-up job of keeping on top of their own grades and classroom standing, but a good rule of thumb is to speak with teachers about your players' standings. Use the start of the school year to exercise prudence in finding out how players perform in class — both academically and attitude-wise. Most faculty appreciate coaches who check up on their athletes. The start of the school year is a good time to set the tone for the coach's involvement in this important issue.

August also is the time of year to check the athletic department closet. Get players to keep inventory of all summer equipment (Form 1, next page). That's no easy process. Check on any new equipment ordered as well (Form 2, page 113).

An important relationship to develop is with a sporting goods dealer or two. Although getting the best deals on athletic equipment usually falls on the athletic director's shoulders, you always should be on the lookout for the best buys.

10.2 Avoiding The Fall Follies

When August wanes and September comes, basketball coaches everywhere start thinking about their seasons. Summer programs are over, camps are done and now coaches turn their full attention to the matter at hand: running

Summer Equipment Inventory Sheet

Equipment	Number we started with	Number we ended with	Condition	Comments on condition

1

their teams.

Fall is a fantastic time of year. School is open again and the excitement and anticipation of starting anew gives everyone a jolt of enthusiasm. However, basketball coaches in particular must be aware of the fall follies — areas of concern that the unsuspecting coach falls prey to, sometimes without even realizing it.

Folly No. 1 — Discouraging your players from participating in fall sports. A common pitfall in many schools is for the basketball coach to discourage players from participating in fall sports. In small schools, especially, limiting athletes' extracurricular activities is a troublesome move. Coaches have a great deal of control of their players, especially the younger ones, and it is disheartening to learn that a fellow coach is telling his athletes not to play another sport. In this country, we have far too much specialization in sports today and the athlete who only plays basketball misses the opportunity to play for other coaches, to stay in shape and to contribute to the overall athletic success of the school. Don't worry about the injury risk and don't worry about other sports taking away from basketball. Players need to taste life on the court and all fields of play.

Folly No. 2 — Letting academics

New Equipment Inventory Sheet

Equipment	Date arrived	Condition of	Other comments

2

slide. Don't wait until winter to track the athletic standing of your players. Granted, basketball coaches must walk a bit of a tightrope in the fall relative to seeking out specific players for grade updates but with veteran coaches who have been in the building for some time, a discreet perusal of marks goes a long way in avoiding academic disaster.

Folly No. 3 — Only concentrating on basketball. One of the best ways to endear yourself to fellow coaches — an important relationship in any school — is to attend games other than your own. Coach snobbery is frowned upon and don't let your players have a perception that you only care about your-

self. Be enthusiastic, helpful and a cheerleader for every other sport your school offers. Even during the winter months, you should find the time to attend the winter track meets or the lower level games in basketball.

Folly No. 4 — Ignoring the details. Basketball's busywork is tedious but fall is the best time to check dates, referee assignments, bus departures, etc. Your athletic director shouldn't put up a gripe as you are reinforcing his or her work. Don't get caught napping. Success is in the details.

Folly No. 5 — Not getting physically and emotionally ready for basketball. Another area often overlooked is preparation for the long season physically and emotionally. Being in good shape takes hours of work. Mental health is enhanced by non-basketball activities. If you as a coach never hit your stride, then chances are good that your team won't hit theirs during the basketball season.

10.3 Avoiding The Parent Trap

August is another good time to assess your relationships with players' parents. Handling parents in this day and age is tricky. Unsuspecting coaches, especially those new to the profession, can get caught in the "parent trap," making commitments they have no business making, dishing out promises they have no business dishing out and generally creating a lot of difficulty. The following are some situations to avoid and solutions to dilemmas that bring coaches to their knees.

Situation No. 1 — Never, ever accept a dinner invitation when you're the only guest. New coaches get dinner invitations in the fall. The parent(s) may sound genuine and sincere but more likely than not they're looking to get in good with you as coach. Socializing with parents and students gives the wrong message to the other kids on your team.

Situation No. 2 — Don't let them bend your ear. Here's a good rule: No parent gets to talk to you about playing time unless you're in the company of the athletic director or another school official. Basketball is not an equal-opportunity employer and you only can put five players on the floor at the same time. Watch out for parents who like to talk. A casual conversation about your team's future quickly could develop into something else. Feel free to talk to parents casually and briefly about the weather, a local college game or your family, but not about the team.

Situation No. 3 — Phone calls are only for emergencies. Tell your players' parents that if you've mishandled a health issue or verbally abuse their child, then they have the right to call you. Your phone shouldn't ring.

Situation No. 4 — Tell players the lineup isn't made at their parents' dinner tables. It's not easy but you must convince your players to listen to you in regard to basketball-related issues and not their parents. Most parents think their child should be on the floor during crunch time. It doesn't work that way. This is your team and your decisions.

10.4 Time For A Vacation?

The summer program is complete. You've spent your time on the camp scene. You've finished meetings with players. Now, it's time for some time away. You don't have to put basketball completely out of your life.

For example, if you have some friends in the coaching profession, go camping, enjoy the rustic offerings and relax by running your own hoops seminar in the wilderness. It provides you with a little camaraderie away from the stress, accompanied by in-depth discussions of several areas of basketball discussion. Or, consider attending a summer one-man clinic. Several well-

["Socializing with parents and students gives the wrong message to the other kids on your team."]

known college coaches (Coach K at Duke and Bobby Knight are examples) have been conducting off-season basketball schools. Put together a group of coaches and take a trip to one of these clinics. Go see a baseball game or a WNBA game along the way.

Or, instead of spending the time with coaches, use part of August to take your team on a non-basketball retreat. Overnight camping, swimming, mountain climbing and the proverbial singing around the campfire goes a long way in developing team unity and cohesiveness. The players get to see you in a different light and it gets them out of the gym.

10.5 Being A Good School Person

Earlier in this chapter, I mentioned attending other sporting events at your school. Extend this into other areas of school activities as well to do even more for your school. Basketball players love it when the coach shows up to one of their events, which are non-basketball related. But a ticket to a school play featuring some of your players. Take a road trip to the school's baseball game. You players will be happy you're there and will work a little harder knowing you're there.

Along with attending other events, take some time to volunteer for supervisory duties at non-basketball events. Principals always are on the lookout for dance chaperones, bus chaperones and other adult supervisory roles that a lot of teachers and coaches shy away from using lack of time as an excuse.

You also could coach a different sport for the school. In small schools coaches are spread too thin sometimes but coaching a different sport might be just what the doctor ordered for you and the school. For example, if the school desperately needs a cross-country coach, consider it. Once again, players get a chance to see you in a different light and maybe you even can convince some of them to come out for the sport. Some running in the fall isn't going to hurt basketball players in the winter.

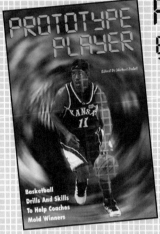

Chapter 11

SEPTEMBER: TIME TO THINK LIKE A COACH AGAIN

11.1 The A, B, C's of Coaching

September is a great time to run through the A, B, C's of coaching.

A. Attitude — You must understand that bringing the proper attitude to the gym begins the first day. De-emphasize winning, teach values and promote teamwork.

B. Basketball — There must be a working knowledge of our game and if you're not comfortable with all the nuances of hoopology, start reading, attending seminars or hanging around those who do.

C. Clinics — A definite, valuable aid to all you do, clinics are the place to frequent if you need everything from a refresher course to a slam dunk in the basics.

D. Defense — An obvious weakness in a lot of coaching circles, knowledge of defensive instruction, especially in man-to-man defense, is lacking in a lot of corners. Don't add yourself to this group. Swallow your pride and learn the game.

E. Effort — The very best of the best in our profession work tirelessly at this game. You'd be wise to count yourself among that group.

F. Fundamentals — School yourself in the basics of the game. Don't get caught in all the new things that come and go. Teach basic individual skills first and watch the team-orientated stuff fall into place.

G. Guards — Guard play for coaches who didn't play that position often is difficult to teach. Embrace the many nuances of playing out front and get help if you don't know what you're talking about.

H. Halftime — Learn early that those brief minutes within a game, if properly used, either solidify what you're doing out there or alter what needs to be changed. Pep talks are all well and good but coaches who adjust well to change generally win.

I. Interaction — Keep your coaches involved in the process by interacting with them constantly. Far too many coaches are stuffy and arrogant about help and change. Don't fall into that conceited category.

[**"Teach basic individual skills first and watch the team-orientated stuff fall into place."**]

J. Jump — Learn the J's of coaching: jumpshots (and how to teach preliminary footwork); jumpstops; and run-and-jump pressure. If you master those, you're well on your way to success and don't forget improving vertical jump for your players.

K. Knowledge — A little bit of knowledge is a dangerous thing, especially if you put off the posture that you know it all. Be a seeker of coaching hoops knowledge every chance you get.

L. Love — Love this game like nothing else in your life, except family, faith and friends, in that order (thank you again, John Wooden).

M. Multiple Defenses — Want to make your team more effective? Teach them a variety of defensive sets to use when moving away from your man defense. This makes you tough to beat.

N. Never — There are several "nevers" in this business: never berate a player in public; never talk about players' weaknesses to the press; never criticize a colleague (we get enough of that from outside sources); and never be unprofessional in the gym or outside of it.

O. Offense — Gear your offense(s) around what your players are able to do. Don't be a stuffed shirt and force kids who can't run to press. Losing usually is the result.

P. Presses — Solid coaches have a variety of pressure defenses in their arsenal. A good place to begin teaching pressure is to employ man-to-man pressure in your system. You're not always going to be ahead in every game.

Q. Quick — Teaching players to be quick is no easy chore but teaching them to be quick thinkers is a must in our game.

R. Rest — Never underestimate the importance of rest to your players. You want them fresh and you also want them to recognize the signs of fatigue within their own bodies.

S. Spacing — If your offensive instruction doesn't include a discussion on spacing, then you need to add this key variable to your list of to-do's.

T. Transition — Transition is not just about getting down the floor to score. Transition from offense to defense is critical and a weak area in many programs. Accent this key variable, then watch your opponent score less.

U. Utility People — Not all players can shoot. Develop a bench by accenting key role players in utility situations. Play more kids. Develop a deeper bench.

V. Varsity — Want a helpful hint for your season? Tell your players that the season is one, long tryout. Never let kids get too comfortable as they will become complacent.

W. Win — Yes, if done properly, all of this leads to winning. Just don't let it be Job No. 1. If you do, other areas falter.

X. X Factor — The X factor, or the unknown, is the nebulous variable of team chemistry. You can't make kids get along but taking them to non-hoop events such as a camping trip aids the development of camaraderie more than anything you do in the gym.

Y. Youth — Never forget the age of

[**"Never berate a player in public; never talk about players' weaknesses to the press..."**]

the participants. Pressure if a tough thing to handle and most small towns expect big things from their teams.

Z. Zealous — Be zealous in your approach to the game but be cautious about being overzealous. Draw the line on those who would go to any length to win a basketball game.

11.2 Trouble Spots

Using time in September to pinpoint potential problem areas saves you headaches when the regular season is in full swing. Pay attention to these problems areas (come up with some solutions) now.

Problem Area No. 1 — Seniors who don't play. Loyalty to the program has to be considered when selecting seniors for your team. A good rule of thumb is to keep kids who help the team, then handle the senior issues individually. Just be cautious of a senior who won't be playing much. It's dangerous to let that individual spread his or her attitude of "I should be playing more," to the rest of the team. In the best of situations, eight (or maybe nine) players get quality time every contest.

Problem Area No. 2 – Assistants who aren't loyal. A troubling situation is when you have an assistant coach who would rather be a head coach than your assistant. A lot of times they give lip services to your desires while doing what they please in their practices and games. Set the tone early that you don't stand for this kind of insubordination. If you don't, it will take longer to clean up their messes than it would to address your demands early.

Problem Area No. 3 — Parents who bother. We covered this already (Chapter 10.3) but it bears repeating

— don't fall prey to a troublesome parent(s). Keep discussions brief, do it on your turf and don't discuss playing time.

Problem Area No. 4 — Players who stretch the rules. There's always a player or two who likes to test the coach's patience by stretching the limits of the simplest rules. To handle this type of player, refer to the rules established in the contract with the player in Chapter 1.7.

Problem Area No. 5 — Grades. Not every player who comes under your watchful eye is headed to West Point but all players need to be held accountable for what happens in the classroom. Keep in touch with faculty and don't treat them like the enemy.

Problem Area No. 6 — Poor fan behavior. It is the job of the athletic administrator and the head coach to educate the general public regarding expectation of behavior while at basketball games. Some schools print a sportsmanship message on their game programs while others go so far as to meet with fans and parents in the pre-season to discuss the school district's stance on such matters. Vulgar, rude treatment of players, the opposition and game officials should not be tolerated at any time.

Problem Area No. 7 — Continuity among support teams. It is your job to ensure proper continuity among lower-level teams. This is best done through constant contact with those teams' coaches. Regular meetings, seminars, notes and appearances go a long way in making for smooth sailing.

11.3 Strengthening Legs

Another important September activity is off-season leg strengthening.

Leg Strengthening Exercise Chart

Exercises	Date	Reps	Right leg Reps	Left leg Reps	Vertical jump before exercise	Vertical jump before exercise
Step-ups						

1

Although this work can happen any time in the off-season, get your players focused on improving their vertical jumps in the fall.

This does not mean spending all of their free time in the weight room. The coach does not have the responsibility to alter body mass. Most of these kids still are in their physical maturation process. You don't want to put them in harm's way.

Leg-strengthening exercises, which do not include weights, are easy to do. Steps are the simplest form of physical improvement work. Pull out a bleacher (or instruct players to use a step at home) and place one foot on the surface, then step up with the other. Reverse the process and do the same thing with the other leg. A good starting point is three sets of five reps for each leg.

Chart vertical jumps before players begin these exercises. Keep track (Form 1) while having players do the step-ups three days per week (rest days are vital).

11.4 Open Gym

As October approaches, non-fall

sports participants and athletes who have finished their regular sports season all want to get back into the gym and play basketball. Be sure this time is used wisely but don't be a part of it yourself — there could be rules violations and if you're already working with players in late September and October, there's a good chance they will get tired of you during the season.

In most states, there is an allowable starting date for the official start of practice. Coaching staffs are not allowed to be involved in a basketball setting until that specific date. So, it becomes important that players are supervised by adults who care about not only their safety but also the organization of play. Unsupervised play is not recommended.

Another factor of open gym to consider is make sure it is not co-ed. Injuries can occur and too much show-ing off spoils the purpose of open gym. Speaking of injuries, tell cross-country and soccer players to be extra careful when hitting the hardwoods after their fall season. Those players usually develop shin splits because they are used to running on soft surfaces, instead of hardwood.

Take the time to whisper in the ears of your captains that if the team is participating in open gym, then the players should make it a worthwhile experience (and play defense while in open gym). There isn't enough time in the preseason to clean up bad habits.

Finally, stress to open-gym participants to take advantage of any time they have to shoot the basketball. Shooting percentages are down these days because players don't put in the individual workout time by shooting the ball.

["Stress to open-gym participants to take advantage of any time they have to shoot the basketball."]

Chapter 12

OCTOBER: PREPARING FOR WHAT LIES AHEAD

12.1 Organizing Your Coaching Staff

An important part of October's preparation period for the beginning of the high school basketball season is coaching staff organization. There are four keys to organizing your staff.

Key No. 1 — Both junior varsity and freshman teams mirror the varsity in all areas. The junior varsity and freshman teams need to be mini-varsity squads. Have these coaches run your primary offense, play man-to-man defense and play every kid in every game.

Key No. 2 — JV and freshman coaches need to attend all varsity practices. There are practices and regular season game scheduling conflicts that may not allow the JV and freshman coaches always to attend your practice. But, it is important for everyone to watch you teach. This helps the lower-level coaches with their practice plans. You also need to demonstrate an interest in what the lower-level teams are doing. On game day, arrive in time to watch the entire JV game and try to see as many freshman games as you can.

Key No. 3 — What about the varsity assistants? If you and your school district can afford a varsity assistant, then this position can provide a valuable link to the head coach. Communication between the two is critical. Pick someone who thinks like you and plans on listening to you. During the season, there's always time for input but little time for argument.

Key No. 4 — Youth programs need to be on the same wavelength with the high school. Middle or junior-high programs are much easier to monitor than the lower levels. The lower levels typically have people who volunteer their time and feel like they can run their teams like a varsity coach would. From an instructional standpoint, the fundamental teaching area going by the wayside is defense. Youth basketball players should be in a man-to-man defense at all times. If they don't learn now, how are they going to fit into your system down the road?

> **"An important part of October's preparation period...is coaching staff organization."**

Coach Self-Evaluation Form

1. What are my strengths? _____

_____

_____

_____

_____

2. What are my weaknesses? _____

_____

_____

_____

_____

3. How do I communicate with my players? _____

_____

_____

_____

_____

4. How do I communicate with my staff: _____

_____

_____

_____

_____

5. How am I perceived around the building? _____

_____

_____

_____

Form continued on next page

1

Coach Self-Evaluation Form (cont.)

6. Areas which I need improvement: _____

_____

_____

_____

_____

7. Am I taking care of business at school? _____

_____

_____

_____

_____

8. Am I taking care of business at home? _____

_____

_____

_____

_____

1

12.2 Self-Evaluation Methods For Coaches

Back in the chapter on May, self-evaluation was discussed (Chapter 7.4). Now, in October, self-evaluation is up for discussion again as you head into the season. Pull out the old form you filled out in May and review it. Also, take the time to reflect on what you expect of yourself with the new season upon you (use Form 1, previous page).

12.3 Preseason Preparations

If you want to be ahead of the game, make your preseason work effective by leaving no stone unturned in the fall.

As November nears, think about checking on players' grades again, working out health issues (players needing physicals, current injuries to players) and alerting any new staff to your expectations and your system.

Also, start to get into a basketball frame of mind in October. Start this process by acquainting yourself with the annual list of rule changes, then move on to the referee points of emphasis. Try watching some preseason NBA games as well. Keep a pad and pen near your television set and take notes on how teams deal with special situations, like end-of-game strate-

Exercise Worksheet

Activity	Date	Minutes Exercised	Hours Exercised	Reps Comments

2

gies, out-of-bounds plays, when to use time-outs, etc.

To be completely ready for the season, make certain you're in good physical health. By nature, a lot of coaches are out of shape. If you're one of them, begin a program you can handle and build up to a level you can sustain. Don't walk into the gym the first night and start playing full-court basketball with tryout participants. Get into a decent physical exercise routine and dietary routine. For those of us over 40, check with your doctor before starting an exercise program.

When you begin an exercising program — start slowly. For example, if you decide to go jogging, don't go for a 5-mile run the first day. You don't need to be injured heading into the season. Take it easy and use jogging to your advantage. It's just you and the roads. Use this time to organize your thoughts, digest the day's happenings and plan for the future. Another good form of exercise is the stationary bike. It gets your heart rate up and keeps you indoors, which is a good thing if you live in a place like Maine. Like jogging, the bike gives you a chance to clear your head. Or, throw in a game film and watch it while on the bike.

Just like everything else, chart your exercising success (Form 2, previous page). This helps significantly as you push for improvement.

If you are in shape for the basketball season, don't hit the court with your players too often. An occasional appearance by the head coach never hurt anyone. But, too many appearances by the coach diminish the necessary distance you need to keep from your players. Coaches who always are running up and down the floor with their teams lose a little something credibility-wise and potentially they open themselves up to comments behind their back. Once a coach loses his or her ability to be productive as a player, then it's time to sit. You're the coach — not one of the kids.

12.4 Scouting Future Players And The Dreaded Opposition

Getting ready for the upcoming sea-son also means getting back into scouting (the opposition and your future players). Now is the time to review some of the basics to scouting.

Arrive at a game early. You'd be surprised what you can pick up just by watching warm-ups. Keep an eye on where certain kids are shooting during a pre-game free-shoot period. Knowing where a player likes to from could be a key component to shutting him down later in the season. Plus, arriving early lets you review the program and find an unobtrusive place to sit.

After the game starts, look for team patterns. Does this team like a motion offense versus man? Do they prefer dropping back into a 2-3 zone out of an even-front zone press?

Also, pay attention to what the team doesn't like. If they aren't comfortable facing a zone, maybe you need to think about showing a zone look at this team when you play them. For example, I was scouting Schenck High School against Central High as we had Schenck coming up in a tourney draw. On one out-of-bound play under Schenck's basket, Central played a 2-3 zone. Schenck fumbled the ball and took a poor shot. When we played Schenck they knew us and knew we played man-to-man defense. We come out in a 2-3 zone and blew them out. One play in 32 minutes of scouting was the key to our success.

"If you are in shape for the basketball season, don't hit the court with your players too often."

Priority Code: Priority Code: WHCDCG

Chapter 13

NOVEMBER: HERE WE GO AGAIN

A finished journey includes a stop back into November. After covering some of the basics in Chapter 1, this chapter covers other areas of importance as you begin your second year of following a calendar coaching guide.

13.1 Keeping The Uniform, Uniform

High school basketball teams should not allow for players to take some creativity in how they look when wearing the team uniform. Strictly speaking, have your players dress the same for all practices and for all games.

A decent, two-color practice uniform is ideal for all players. Most kids and parents financially can meet this obligation. If your school can afford a full practice uniform, then make sure your players respect practice gear as much as they respect the school uniform. And, be sure all shirts are tucked in at all times. Begin by teaching uniform habits in practice and it carries over to games.

When it comes to game uniforms, start with a decision on game socks. Keep socks the same and if you want, have the team vote on a certain style of sock. As for shoes, budget constraints make it much more difficult to put

everyone in the same pair of sneakers but nothing looks sharper than a group of players who are dressed the same from top to bottom. If your team does go to the shoe store together, be sure each player is measured individually. Kids notoriously have wide or narrow feet and would be better-served with a different brand of shoe. Color schemes can be imitated to accommodate a different shoe.

Another area to discuss is the use of headbands and wristbands. This is an area of difference for boys and girls. If all girls are wearing something on their head, be sure everyone is wearing the same color. If boys want to wear headbands or wrist bands for no other purpose than style — outlaw them.

Many schools now are going to a travel suit for when teams go on the road. Budget constraints again come into play and if just one player can't afford to purchase the suit, no one should buy one. Some schools may have the budget to purchase these suits for players. If so, be sure everyone is looking the same and no one has decided to change the suit to fit their "style."

After establishing all types of gear players are wearing, set some guidelines of school-issued clothing. Let players take practice gear home with them. It's too time-consuming to distribute and collect this gear everyday. But, for school uniforms, distribute them that day and collect them at the end of the game. Buy a trunk and have a manager assume the responsibility of upkeep and distribution, so it's one less thing on your mind.

13.2 Pinpoint Your Weaknesses Early

One of the toughest jobs facing coaches today is pinpointing weaknesses and attacking them. Many coaches spend preseason time on brushing up on areas where the team excels hoping that when weaknesses arise, the team has the ability to slide by. Don't wait to address weaknesses. They catch up with you quickly. There are some common areas where teams struggle.

Area No. 1 — Half-court traps. It takes a decent club to thwart pressure but you should have enough weapons to combat all types of pressure with half-court traps being no exception. Always leave a guard behind a trap as a safety valve. Leaving the responsibility of breaking traps to one kid is unfair. Always keep your best ball catcher in the middle of the floor, flashing to help. Always have a plan in mind to score behind the trap, whether off a baseline flash or a corner shot. Failing to attack traps often ends up in a game of lob-pass keep-away, which rarely works.

Area No. 2 — Man defense. Don't use the excuse that your team doesn't match up well or isn't really adept at playing single-coverage defense. Man-to-man defense should be a staple at the high-school level. Zones have their place but teaching your kids good half-court man-to-man is as fundamental to your

success as proper shooting techniques.

Area No. 3 — Special situations. Special situations must not be ignored. Everything from clock-management to end-game strategies fall into this category. This area is addressed further a little later in this chapter.

Area No. 4 — Point guard problems. Point guards are not a dime a dozen. A good testing ground for point guards is to run preseason drills that put guards or guard candidates under pressure in the half-court and see who is successful versus presses, the double-team or zone traps. Sometimes your best player for this role is a player in a different position.

13.3 Special Situations Need Special Time

It's difficult to cover all your bases. Many times, special situations take a backseat to teaching offense and defense. Special situations include any element of basketball transpiring away from the normal flow of the game. Examples include: out-of-bounds plays; all types of pressure; and end-game strategies. Coaches who wing it in these situations are doing a disservice to their players. Enter the gymnasium thinking your players want to learn all things and leave no stone unturned.

It's amazing how so many teams put so little emphasis on in-bounding the ball under their own basket. The main focus of in-bounding the ball under your own basket is not to score but to get the ball in-bounds within five seconds. Tell your players this every day. They need to know that scoring is not the top priority.

Another tip is to have the majority of what you do under your basket look the same, then end differently. Also, never draw up a play on a whim during a game. Only uses out-of-bounds plays players have practiced. In the frenzy of a game, it's not fair to expect your players quickly to focus, process and perform something they haven't practiced. When the time comes to run an in-bound play, watch the defense's positioning. At this point, communicate with your in-bounder who then communicates the play to everyone else.

The first set of diagrams focuses on specific out-of-bounds plays against zones.

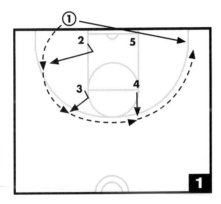

DIAGRAM 1: In-Bound Vs. Even-Front Zone. Attack the zone with a 1-2-2 box. 1 passes to 2, who made a V-cut to get open. 3 makes a V-cut on the wing, then receives the pass from 2. 4 pops out to the 3-point area and receives a pass from 3. The goal is to get the ball back to 1, who is going to rub a defender off 5 to get open for a corner shot.

DIAGRAM 2: Wrinkle To Diagram 1. To fool the defense, set up in the same 1-2-2 box as Diagram 1. Again, 1 passes to 2, who made a V-cut to get open. 3 makes a V-cut as before and receives a pass from 2. 3 then makes a hard ball-fake to 4 and passes back to 1, who has hesitated but has come in-bound as 2 makes his way

back to the block.

Against a man-to-man defense, put all four players in a line at the foul line. A slap of the ball initiates the play.

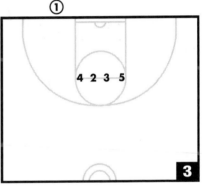

DIAGRAM 3: Stack Vs. Man-To-Man. 1 is the in-bounder. 4, 2, 3 and 5 line up in a stack at the foul line.

DIAGRAM 4: Initial Play Vs.

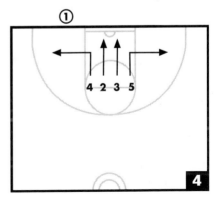

Man-To-Man. 1 slaps the ball to initiate the play. All players cut into the lane. 4 and 5 pop out to their side after their initial cut.

If you have a hot shooter, use this stack to get him an open shot. Diagram 5 shows how this is done.

DIAGRAM 5: In-Bound Play For Hot Shooter. If 3 is your hot shooter, use a triple screen to free him. 3 steps back. 4, 2 and 5 move closer. 1 passes to 3. If the defense cheats, then move to Diagram 6.

DIAGRAM 6: Beating A Cheating Defense. If X3 cheats and jumps the play, 3 cuts to the hoop for an easy catch and score.

When in-bounding the ball from the sideline, use a line formation. 2 and 3 are the best ball-handlers.

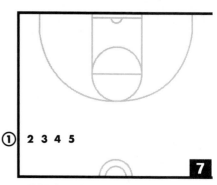

DIAGRAM 7: Sideline In-Bound Set-Up.

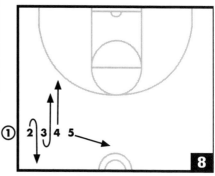

DIAGRAM 8: Motion Out Of Line Formation. 1 slaps the ball to initiate the play. 2 and 3 fake cut in opposite directions, then cut the other way. 4 and 5 are safety valves.

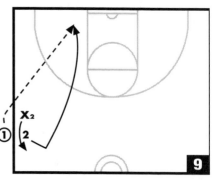

DIAGRAM 9: Beat An Overplaying Defense. If X2 tries to jump the play and beat 2 to his spot, 2

cuts long to the hoop for an easy in-bound catch.

Instead of a line series on a sideline in-bound situation, try a shuffle side-line series. If motion offense is your primary offense, the shuffle sideline series is a good one to use.

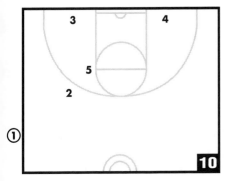

DIAGRAM 10: Alignment In Shuffle Series. 1 is your point guard. 1 normally is in control of your offense, so it makes sense he or she is your in-bounder. An initial move out of this for-mation is to have 2 make a V-cut to get open. If this works, 2 usually can get the ball back to 1. Also, teach your players to keep an eye on 4. Many times, teams don't pay attention to this player as he appears to be out of the action. If 4 is unguarded, have him flash from the corner to about three-quarters of the way across the lane.

Special Situation No. 2 — Press breakers. The most important thing about breaking pressure successfully is to teach your players to take their time. No matter if it's man-to-man pressure or zone pressure, patience is the key. Against man pressure, keep the ball in

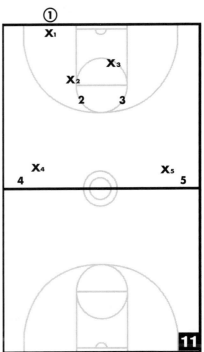

your best ball-handler's hands as much as possible. Against zone, advance the ball up the floor by passing.

DIAGRAM 11: Initial Set-Up Vs. Man Pressure. 1 is your point guard. 2 and 3 are your other solid ball-han-dlers. 2 and 3 should try to rub their defenders off one another to get open. If 2 or 3 receives the in-bound pass, they should look to pass the ball back to 1 if possible. Discourage 2 or 3 from dribbling against the pressure. If the ball gets back to 1, 1 brings the ball up and begins the offense. Keep a guard back (2 or 3) in case of a trap.

If the defense does trap or double-team, players need to be ready. Diagram 12 illustrates how to combat a trap after

["The most important thing about breaking pressure successfully is to teach your players to take their time."]

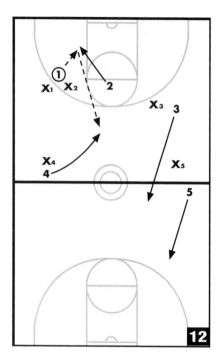

1 has the ball back in his hands.

DIAGRAM 12: Beating The Trap. 2 stays back to help 1 in case of a trap. In this instance, X1 and X2 trap 1. 1 passes back to 2. 4 cuts to the middle of the court. 2 passes to 4 as 3 and 5 sprint toward the basket, looking for a pass from 4 for a fast-break score. If this is not available, 4 looks to get the ball back into 1's hands.

When a team shows full-court zone pressure, the primary objective is to keep the ball off the floor as much as possible. Diagram 13 shows an initial alignment against a 1-2-1-1 zone press. Notice how the set-up is the same as facing a man-to-man press.

DIAGRAM 13: Alignment Vs. 1-2-1-1 Zone Pressure.

DIAGRAM 14: Attacking A 1-2-1-1 Zone Press. 1 in-bounds to 2. 5 flashes to the middle of the court and

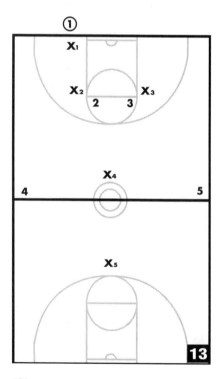

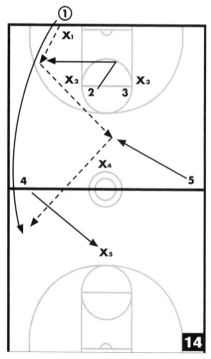

receives a pass from 2. After throwing the in-bound pass, 1 streaks up the near sideline. 5 passes to 1. Notice how there is no dribbling in this attack.

Special Situation No. 3 — Endgame. Don't hope for a lucky play or a desperate game-winning shot at the end of a game. Be prepared for these situations as well. When you're in-bounding under your own basket for the last shot, focus on having a play that looks the same but finishes differently. For example, say you've been back-picking for 5 all day on a similar in-bound scenario, like in Diagram 15.

DIAGRAM 15: Back-Pick For 5. 2 goes from his spot on the block to the opposite wing to back-pick for 5, who then is open for an easy lay-up.

If you've run this play enough dur-

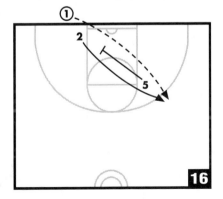

ing the game, come out in the same set-up at the end of the game, then add a wrinkle.

DIAGRAM 16: Fake Back-Pick. Have 2 move toward the opposite wing to make his back-pick and have 5 flash across the lane and cut to the hoop. But, instead of 2 stopping where he would make his screen, he continues out to the 3-point line. 1 passes to 2 and 2 shoots the final shot.

Many times, you have the ball in the half-court set for the final shot. Keep the ball in your point guard's hands as much as possible. Let your point guard create a final shot. Here's a play against a man-to-man defense from the stack series outlined in Chapter 1.

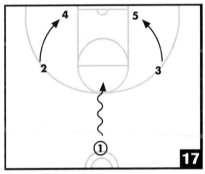

DIAGRAM 17: Setting Up The Stack. As 1 begins to penetrate, 2 and 3 drop to the post behind the larger 4 and 5.

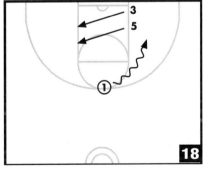

DIAGRAM 18: Initial Movement

In Stack. If 1 is right-handed, he dribbles right. 3 and 5 move out of the way to the opposite side of the lane. Allow 1 to create his or her last shot.

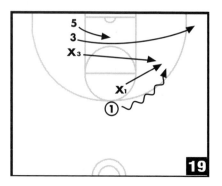

DIAGRAM 19: Helping After The Stack. If 1's movement is stopped by a defender, have 5 rotate back to the lane. If 3's defender came to help on 1, have 3 cross to the corner for a possible last shot. 2 and 4 also need to be moving on the other side of the floor to get open. In last-shot situations, all players need to stay active in trying to get open.

Sometimes you need to go the length of the court for a final shot. Have your point guard in-bound the ball and immediately receive a pass back. The point guard then should advance the ball with the dribble. You would be surprised how the defense shies away from the point guard so as not to foul. Now the ball is in the front court and you are in business. However, if there are only two or three seconds left in the game and you need to go 84 feet to win, bring your biggest player as far up the court as he needs to go to receive a pass. Have your remaining players fan out around the court for a possible final shot.

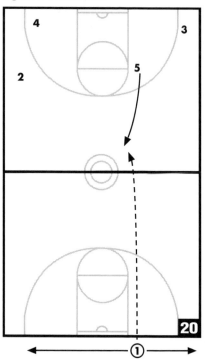

DIAGRAM 20: Last-Second Full-Court Shot Scenario. 1 runs the baseline to get the best look (if off a made shot). 5 flashes toward midcourt to receive a pass. 2, 3 and 4 fan out and try to get open for a final shot. Depending on how many points you need, 5 looks to the according player (if you need 3 points, 5 looks for 3 or 2).

13.4 Drills To Teach The System

One of the most important aspects of teaching basketball is drill instruction and November is a perfect time for drills. You need to develop good practice

[**"In last-shot situations, all players need to stay active in trying to get open."**]

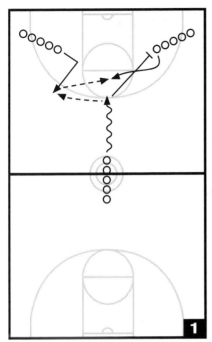

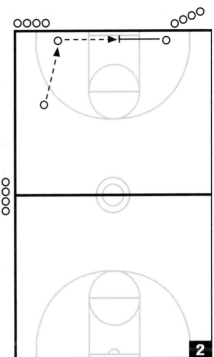

drills to keep your players interested. Drills should be designed for offense, defense and individual instruction.

Drill Area No. 1 — Drills for offense. Developing skills such as passing, cross-screening and finding open shooters are not to be taken lightly.

DRILL 1: Perimeter Shooting. One player starts at half-court, dribbles to the top of the 3-point area, passes to a player in the line to the left, then screens for a player in a line to the right. The player on the left who caught the pass waits for the screen to be set, then passes to the player from the right who is flashing toward the free-throw line area. Run this drill on both ends of the floor in tryouts and when combining JV and varsity practices. Also, stress players setting legal screens and make proper jab steps. Chart progress (Form 1, next page).

DRILL 2: Power Lay-Up. The player in the backcourt passes to a player on the same side in the frontcourt. The player from the opposite side of the floor makes a three-quarter cut across the lane and receives a pass from the frontcourt player. Stress players making a strong three-quarter cut across the lane.

Both of these drills are fundamental enough to run all the time but contain enough details to be able to distinguish players who understand the concepts and those who don't. Use the forms on the following two pages to chart player progress for these two drills.

Drill Area No. 2 — Drills for defense. A lot of coaches love using a version of the age-old zig-zag drill because it teaches footwork, sliding, hustling to recover, stance and attitude. Use coaches as passers to initiate the drill. Chart progress (Form 2, page 139).

Perimeter Shooting Drill Chart

Player's name: _____

Date	Number of shots attempted	Number of shots made

1

DRILL 3: Zig-Zag. The coach inbounds the ball to the offensive player. The defender steps up and slides while playing solid defense. The defender can try to steal the ball but no reaching or grabbing is allowed. Have the drill continue all the way down the floor. Make it competitive by charting who did the best job on offense and defense. The following two forms show how to

CALENDAR COACHING GUIDE

Power Lay-Up Drill Chart

Player's name: _____

Date	Number of shots attempted	Number of shots made

2

chart this drill (Form 3-4, next pages).

To drill your players against the run-and-jump defense, use the next drill. It has one dribbler get by a defender only to be met by another.

DRILL 4: Run-And-Jump. The dribbler comes from the baseline to meet one defender. After getting by that defender, another from mid-court comes to meet the dribbler.

Drill Area No. 3 — Drills for the individual. Rebounding, ball-handling and shooting are key areas to drill individuals.

Try to teach your rebounding drills with verbal and physical components. When a shot is taken be sure players scream "SHOT!" and everyone throws their arms in the air. You'd be surprised at how many rebounds hit those outstretched arms.

DRILL 5: Rebounding Drill On Player Shot. The offensive player dribbles from the mid-court area on one side of the floor. The player stops and shoots from the free-throw line. The defender yells "SHOT!" and boxes out the offensive player for the rebound. The offensive player goes after his own shot.

DRILL 6: Rebounding Drill On Coach Shot. Have you or one of your assistants take a shot from the top of the key. Offensive players come in

Zig-Zag Drill Chart — Offense

Player's name: _____

Date	Strong-hand scores	Off-hand scores	Alternating hands scores	Comments

3

from the sideline while defenders come out from the baseline. Both battle for rebounding position.

When it comes to ball-handling, have players perform maneuver-type drills, especially early in the season.

DRILL 7: Full-Court Ball-Handling. Place chairs spaced out in a line the length of the floor on both sides of the floor (next page). Players

Zig-Zag Drill Chart — Defense

Player's name: _____

Date	Steals vs. strong hand	Steals vs. weak hand	Steals vs. alternating hands	Fouls committed during drill	Balance & defensive technique - rated 1-10 1 = poor 10 = excellent

4

dribble to the first chair with their strong hand, then switch to their weak hand until the next chair. Time this drill and chart it like in Form 5 (page 143).

When you teaching shooting, break it down into three primary areas: perimeter shooting, inside shooting and foul shooting. Be sure to stress foot-work when teaching shooting as foot-work woes plague a lot of shooters. Feet are underrated as an important body part in shooting instruction.

DRILL 8: Circle Drill. For foot-work, have player aligned in a circle at each end of the floor. Blow the whistle, which indicates players take short,

["When it comes to ball-handling, have players perform maneuver-type drills, especially early in the season."]

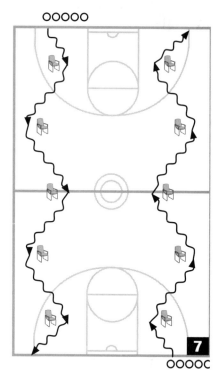

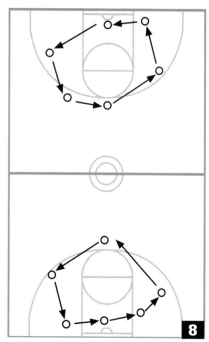

choppy steps to the right. Blow the whistle again to have player drive their inside foot (left foot) down and bring the other foot around, concentrating on being square to the target. Once players have mastered the footwork, extend the drill so they progress up the body to the point of release. Also, go in the reverse direction with this drill so players get used to planting and squaring to the hoop in the other direction. Plus, this keeps lefties happy.

After footwork, players should progress to the 30-second drill, which is having one shooter and one rebounder on the floor. The goal is to see how many makes the shooter can hit in a 30-second span from around the key area. On the whistle, the rebounder fires a pass to the shooter on the perimeter and the shooter takes his first shot. The rebounder is critical in this drill as he must hit the shooter with the type of pass to allow the shooter to square up and shoot. Run this drill every day and be sure players are at different baskets on different days, so they don't get accustomed to shooting at just one hoop. Once again, chart progress (Form 6, page 142) and see how many good baskets a shooter can make. Make this into a competition for the day or for the season.

For inside shooting, begin with footwork again with the age-old Mikan Drill, named for George Mikan, the first great center in the NBA. The drill

[**"Feet are underrated as an important body part in shooting instruction."**]

Ball-Handling Drill Chart — Chart Drill

Player's name: _____

Date	Time with strong hand	Time with off-hand	Time with alternating hand

5

has one player at each basket shooting and retrieving his or her own shot without having the ball touch the floor. Work on lay-ups and hook shots, concentrating on planting on the left foot for a right-handed shot and the right foot for a left-handed shot. Don't time this drill and have players concentrate solely on technique.

As for free-throw shooting, more always is better. There's a famous story of a former Narraguagus High School (Harrington, Maine) player, Gladys Ganiel, who began each school day with a 500-shot free-throw drill routine. She would arrive at school in the early-morning hours and would shoot until she missed. Then, she would start over until she made the next number of consecutive shots she just accomplished. Then, she'd continue on the same routine. Her best consecutive total was 253. Ganiel went on to win four straight state titles as a foul shooter, which just goes to show that free-throw shooting is work.

While you can't expect all of your players to do this kind of work, have them concentrate on proper form and routine when shooting at practice. If they take a breath, dribble the ball

30-Second Drill Chart - Outside Shooting

Name	Date	Number of makes in 30-seconds

6

three times and shoot — that's acceptable and they should be doing this on each free throw. Also, have your players visualize taking 50 free throws before they shut their eyes at night. Visualizing success on every shot trains their brains to know what success is.

13.5 A Final Word

As this book wraps up, there are a few final words to keep in mind as you go on your way. Always treat coaching as a sacred task. Parents allow their offspring to you for an extended period of time — that's a privilege.

Also, young people are like sponges and coaches must be aware that every thought and deed are being watched and imitated — be a good role model.

Basketball really is the best teaching sport as it places participants in a heated environment and forces them to make decisions under pressure in front of hundreds, even thousands, of spectators. The game is like life and how players react to certain situations (like a bad call by a referee) goes a long way in determining how they are to act in life situations. There's nothing greater than watching young people mature into young adults under your supervision.